Paul- The Many Roles of a Servant of Christ

Joshua Rhoades

Published by Joshua Paul Rhoades, 2024.

While every precaution has been taken in the preparation of this book, the publisher assumes no responsibility for errors or omissions, or for damages resulting from the use of the information contained herein.

PAUL- THE MANY ROLES OF A SERVANT OF CHRIST

First edition. October 24, 2024.

Copyright © 2024 Joshua Rhoades.

ISBN: 979-8227086877

Written by Joshua Rhoades.

Also by Joshua Rhoades

Courage Under Fire: David's Stand On The Battlefield
Jonah's Journey: Voices Of Redemption And Lessons In Obedience
The Furnace Of Faith: 12 Principles From The Heat Of Faith
Whispers of Hope: Inspiring Stories of Men's Prayers In Scripture
Frontier Legends: The Oregon Dream
Elijah: A Beacon Of Boldness
HOOK, LINE & SAVIOUR - Faith Reflections from Fishing
Driven By Faith: Motor Racing Inspired Christian Life
30 Day Devotional - Bold and Strong- Coffee Devotions for a Courageous
Christian Walk
Authentic Christianity: The Heart of Old Time Religion
Consider The Ant - God's Tiny Preachers
Flee Fornication: The Plea For Purity
Renewed Hope- How to Find Encouragement in God
Sounding The Call - The Voice of Conviction
The Altar - Where Heaven Meets Earth
The Bible's Battlefields- Timeless Lessons from Ancient Wars
The Sacred Art of Silence - How Silence Speaks in Scripture
Under Fire- The Sanctity of the Traditional Biblical Home
Who Is on the Lord's Side? A Call to Righteousness
What Is Truth? - From Skepticism to Submission
First and Goal- Faith and Football Fundamentals
From Dugout to Devotion- Spiritual Lessons from Baseball
Par for the Course- Faith and Fairways
The Believer's Pace- Tools for Running Life's Marathon
The Immutable Fortress- Security in God's Unchanging Nature
Biblical Bravery
Deer Stands and Devotions: A Hunter's Walk with God

Jesus Knows- Our Hearts, Our Responsibility
Restoration - Setting The Bone
Spiritual 911- God's Word for Life's Emergency's
The Freedom of Forgiveness
The Jezebel Effect - Ancient Manipulations Modern Lessons
The Shout That Stopped The Saviour
The Time Machine Chronicles: Old Testament Characters
Anchored In Truth Exploring The Depths of Psalm 119
Biblical Counsel on Anger
Proverbs' Portraits The Men God Mentions
Stumbling in the Dark - The Dangers of Alcohol
Guarding the Wicket Protecting Your Faith and Game
The Champion's Faith - Wrestling and Achieving Spiritual Victory
Scriptural Commands for Modern Times Living God's Word Today Volume 1
Scriptural Commands for Modern Times Living God's Word Today Volume 2
Scriptural Commands for Modern Times Living God's Word TodayVolume3
The Greatest Gift
A Christmas Journey of Faith
Daughter Of The King: Embracing Your Identity In Christ
Determination and Dedication Building Strong Faith As A Young Man
Walking Through Walls God's Power to Part the Storms of Life
David's Song Of Deliverance Praising God Through Every Storm
From Weakness to Warrior: Gideon's Transformation
Why Did Jesus Weep?
Living For God The Call To Be A Living Sacrifice
My Mind Is In A Fog What Do I Do?
Turning The Page Written By Grace
The Calling and Greatness of John the Baptist
For Such a Time Esther's Courageous Stand
From Brokenness To Beauty Written By The Pen of Grace
The Ultimate Guide to Massive Action- From Plans to Reality
A Heart Of Conviction
Serving In The Shadows
Repentance Revealed The Road Back To God
The Chief Sinner Meets The Chief Saviour Reflections On I Timothy 1:15

Answer The Call - 31 Days of Biblical Action
The Birthmark of the Believer
Reflections on Calvary's Cross
The Kingdom Builder Paul's Bold Proclamation of Christ
The Animal Of Pride
The Reach That Restores Christ Love For The Broken
Paul- The Many Roles of a Servant of Christ

Dedication

This book, "Paul: The Many Roles of a Servant of Christ", is dedicated to your journey—your faith, your calling, and your unique place in the story that God is still writing. As you open these pages, you're stepping into the life of a man whose transformation from persecutor to apostle changed the world. Yet, this is not just Paul's story; it's yours, too. It's about how God can take an ordinary person, regardless of their past, and use them in extraordinary ways. You may not feel like a hero of faith, or you might be wondering if your life can truly make a difference. But just as God used Paul in so many different roles, He can and will use you in ways beyond what you could ever imagine.

Paul's journey is a testament to the incredible things that happen when we surrender ourselves fully to Christ. His life wasn't easy—he faced hardship, rejection, imprisonment, and suffering—but through it all, his love for Jesus and his passion for the Gospel never wavered. In the same way, you might be facing trials, doubts, or moments when you feel like giving up. But remember, God is not looking for perfection; He's looking for a heart that's willing. Paul's roles as a preacher, teacher, shepherd, and defender of the faith show us that every step, every struggle, and every victory in our lives has a purpose in God's plan.

This book is dedicated to you because, like Paul, you have a calling. You have roles to play in God's story that no one else can fill. Maybe you're called to be a teacher, guiding others in the truth of God's Word. Maybe you're a shepherd, nurturing the people in your life with love and care. Perhaps you're called to be a defender of the faith, standing firm in a world that often opposes the truth. Or maybe you're in a season of suffering, feeling like a prisoner of your circumstances, yet your witness, even in pain, can inspire others to see the strength of God in you.

Paul reminds us that we don't have to be perfect to be used by God. In fact, it's through our weaknesses, our past mistakes, and our imperfections that God's grace shines the brightest. So, this dedication is not just to honor Paul's life, but to honor yours—the life you've lived, the faith you carry, and the servant's heart that continues to grow within you. Wherever you are in your journey, know that you are not alone. God is with you, guiding you, shaping you, and calling you to step into the fullness of who He created you to be.

As you read about the many roles Paul played in the early church, may you be encouraged to embrace the roles God has for you. May you see yourself in Paul's story and find the courage to walk boldly in your calling. This book is dedicated to your journey of faith, and my prayer is that through these pages, you will discover more of who God is and more of who He has called you to be. Like Paul, you are a servant of Christ, and your life can and will make a lasting impact for His glory.

Introduction

In "Paul: The Many Roles of a Servant of Christ", we explore the incredible life of the Apostle Paul, a man whose deep love for Jesus Christ shaped the early church and continues to inspire Christians today. Paul's journey was one of transformation, from being a persecutor of Christians to becoming one of the most influential leaders in Christian history. Throughout his ministry, Paul filled many roles that reflect his unwavering commitment to Christ and the spreading of the Gospel. As the Apostle to the Gentiles (Romans 11:13), Paul broke new ground by sharing the message of salvation with non-Jewish communities, helping the Gospel reach people from every nation. As a Preacher of the Gospel (1 Timothy 2:7), Paul boldly proclaimed the good news of Jesus' death and resurrection, often facing persecution and imprisonment but never wavering in his mission. His role as a Servant of Jesus Christ (Romans 1:1) showed his deep humility and dedication to following God's will, always putting the work of the Lord above his own desires. Paul was also a Teacher of the Gentiles (2 Timothy 1:11), helping new believers grow in their faith and understand the transformative power of grace. As a Defender of the Faith (Philippians 1:7), he stood firmly against false teachings and strived to preserve the purity of the Gospel message. Paul served as a Shepherd of the Flock (Acts 20:28), caring deeply for the churches he established, offering guidance, support, and correction when needed. He was a Builder on Christ, the Foundation (1 Corinthians 3:11), ensuring that every church he planted was built on the unshakable truth of Jesus Christ. Additionally, Paul was a Prisoner of Christ (Philemon 1:9), often writing letters of encouragement and instruction from prison, showing that no earthly chains could hinder his devotion to spreading the Gospel. He took on the role of a Spiritual Warrior (Ephesians 6:12), reminding believers that they were in a spiritual battle and equipping them with the armor of God. As a Proclaimer of God's Grace (Acts

20:24), Paul constantly preached the message that salvation comes through faith in Christ alone, not through works. He was also a Persecutor Turned Apostle (1 Corinthians 15:9), demonstrating the power of God's grace to transform even the most unlikely individuals into vessels for His work. Paul's life and ministry were filled with these and many other roles that reflect his dedication to building the early church and helping believers grow in their relationship with God. In this book, we will explore over 20 of these roles, showing how each one contributed to Paul's lasting legacy as a true servant of Christ, whose life continues to inspire Christians around the world to follow Jesus with the same passion, courage, and faith.

Chapter 1 - Apostle to the Gentiles

The Apostle Paul, in Romans 11:13, declares, "For I speak to you Gentiles, inasmuch as I am the apostle of the Gentiles, I magnify mine office." This statement is both profound and powerful, revealing Paul's unique calling and the depth of his dedication to his mission. To understand the weight of these words, we must first grasp the incredible journey of Paul, a man once known as Saul, a fierce persecutor of Christians, transformed by the grace of Jesus Christ to become the chosen vessel through which God's message of salvation would be carried to the Gentiles—the non-Jewish people who were previously considered far from the promises of God. This title, "Apostle to the Gentiles," is not just a mere label; it encapsulates Paul's entire life and ministry, his trials, triumphs, and the deep love he had for those who were once seen as outsiders to the covenant promises of God.

In Paul's time, there was a deep divide between Jews and Gentiles. The Jews, as God's chosen people, had been the recipients of His laws, His prophets, and His covenant. They were the nation through which the Messiah, Jesus Christ, would come. The Gentiles, on the other hand, were seen as strangers to the covenants of promise, as Paul later describes in Ephesians 2:12. They were without Christ, without hope, and without God in the world. But when Jesus came, He fulfilled the law and the prophets, breaking down the "middle wall of partition" (Ephesians 2:14) that had separated Jews and Gentiles. Through His death and resurrection, Jesus made it possible for all people—Jew and Gentile alike—to come to God through faith in Him. This was the heart of the Gospel message that Paul was called to proclaim.

Paul's conversion, recorded in Acts 9, was nothing short of miraculous. He had been a zealous Pharisee, passionately persecuting Christians, believing that he was doing God's will by stamping out what he saw as a dangerous heresy. But on the road to Damascus, Paul encountered the risen Christ, and everything changed. Blinded by a brilliant light and hearing the voice of Jesus asking, "Saul, Saul, why persecutest thou me?" (Acts 9:4), Paul was confronted with the truth that the very Messiah he had been fighting against was, in fact, the Lord. From that moment on, Paul's life took a dramatic turn. Jesus told him that he was a chosen vessel to bear His name "before the Gentiles, and kings, and the children of Israel" (Acts 9:15).

Paul's calling as the Apostle to the Gentiles was not an easy one. He faced opposition from every side. From the Jews, who saw him as a traitor for preaching to the Gentiles and for teaching that salvation came not through the law but through faith in Christ, and from the Gentiles themselves, many of whom mocked and rejected the message of a crucified and risen Savior. Yet, Paul remained steadfast. He endured beatings, imprisonment, shipwrecks, and countless hardships, all for the sake of spreading the Gospel to those who had never heard it before. His love for the Gentiles was evident in everything he did. He longed for them to know the same grace and mercy that had transformed his own life.

The significance of Paul's title, "Apostle to the Gentiles," is rooted in the fact that God's plan of salvation was always meant to extend beyond the borders of Israel. From the very beginning, God's promise to Abraham was that through his seed, "all the families of the earth" would be blessed (Genesis 12:3). Yet, for centuries, the focus had been on Israel as God's chosen people. It was through Israel that God revealed His laws, His prophets, and ultimately, His Messiah. But with the coming of Christ, the time had come for that promise to be fulfilled in a new and greater way. Jesus Himself had hinted at this during His earthly ministry, telling His disciples that they would be His witnesses "in Jerusalem, and in all Judaea, and in Samaria, and unto the uttermost part of the earth" (Acts 1:8). But it was Paul who would take the lead in carrying the Gospel to the Gentiles.

Paul's ministry to the Gentiles was groundbreaking in many ways. He traveled extensively, visiting cities across the Roman Empire, preaching the Gospel and establishing churches. His letters, many of which make up a large portion of the New Testament, were written to these Gentile churches, instructing them in the faith, encouraging them to stand firm in the face of persecution, and explaining the deep theological truths of the Gospel. Paul was not just a preacher; he was a pastor, a teacher, and a father figure to these young churches. He poured out his heart in his letters, often expressing his deep love and concern for them. In 1 Thessalonians 2:7-8, he writes, "But we were gentle among you, even as a nurse cherisheth her children: so being affectionately desirous of you, we were willing to have imparted unto you, not the gospel of God only, but also our own souls, because ye were dear unto us."

One of the central themes of Paul's ministry to the Gentiles was the idea of unity in Christ. In a world divided by ethnicity, social status, and religious backgrounds, Paul preached that in Christ, all those barriers were broken down. In Galatians 3:28, he famously declares, "There is neither Jew nor Greek, there is neither bond nor free, there is neither male nor female: for ye are all one in Christ Jesus." This was a radical message in Paul's time, and it remains a radical message today. The Gospel is the great equalizer. It doesn't matter where you come from, what your background is, or what you have done in the past—through faith in Christ, we are all made one, all part of the same body, the same family of God.

Paul's passion for the Gentiles is also seen in his deep theological reflections on the nature of God's grace. In his letter to the Romans, particularly in chapters 9-11, Paul wrestles with the question of how God's plan for Israel fits with His plan for the Gentiles. He concludes that God's grace is so vast, so incredible, that it encompasses both Jews and Gentiles. He writes, "For God hath concluded them all in unbelief, that he might have mercy upon all" (Romans 11:32). Paul understood that God's plan of salvation was far bigger than anyone had imagined. It wasn't just for one nation, but for all people, Jew and Gentile alike. And this realization filled Paul with awe and wonder. At the end of his theological argument, he breaks out into a doxology, exclaiming, "O the depth of the riches both of the wisdom and knowledge of God! how unsearchable are his judgments, and his ways past finding out!" (Romans 11:33).

Paul's role as the Apostle to the Gentiles was not just a title; it was his life's mission. He gave everything—his time, his energy, his very life—to see that the Gospel reached those who had never heard it before. In 2 Timothy 4:6-7, as Paul nears the end of his life, he reflects on his ministry, saying, "For I am now ready to be offered, and the time of my departure is at hand. I have fought a good fight, I have finished my course, I have kept the faith." Paul's life was one of complete dedication to the cause of Christ. He was not content to sit back and let others do the work; he was driven by a deep sense of responsibility and love for the Gentiles, whom he saw as his spiritual children.

Paul's ministry to the Gentiles also serves as a powerful example of how God can use anyone, no matter their past, for His glory. Paul was once a persecutor of the church, a man who sought to destroy the very thing he would later give his life to build. But God, in His infinite grace, chose Paul, transformed him, and used him in a mighty way. Paul himself never forgot this. He often referred to himself as the least of the apostles, not worthy to be called an apostle because of his past (1 Corinthians 15:9). Yet, he also recognized that it was by the grace of God that he was what he was, and that God's grace toward him was not in vain (1 Corinthians 15:10). Paul's life is a testimony to the fact that no one is beyond the reach of God's grace. No matter how far we have strayed, no matter what we have done, God can redeem us, transform us, and use us for His purposes.

As the Apostle to the Gentiles, Paul's legacy continues to impact the world today. The churches he established, the letters he wrote, and the Gospel he preached have shaped the course of Christian history. His teachings on grace, faith, and the unity of the body of Christ continue to inspire and challenge believers around the world. Paul's life was a life lived for others. He gave everything he had to see that the Gentiles, who were once "strangers and foreigners" to the promises of God, could now be "fellowcitizens with the saints, and of the household of God" (Ephesians 2:19).

In conclusion, Paul's title as the "Apostle to the Gentiles" is more than just a designation; it reflects his deep love for the Gentiles and his unwavering commitment to the Gospel. His life and ministry demonstrate the power of God's grace, the importance

of unity in Christ, and the incredible impact one person can have when they fully surrender to God's call. Paul's legacy as the Apostle to the Gentiles is a reminder to us all that God's love knows no boundaries, that His grace is available to all, and that He can use even the most unlikely people to accomplish His purposes. Through Paul's ministry, the world learned that in Christ, there is no distinction between Jew and Gentile, bond and free, male and female, but all are one in Him. And that message of unity, hope, and salvation continues to resonate today, inspiring us to carry the Gospel to the ends of the earth, just as Paul did so many centuries ago.

Chapter 2 - Preacher of the Gospel

In 1 Timothy 2:7, Paul boldly declares, "Whereunto I am ordained a preacher, and an apostle, (I speak the truth in Christ, and lie not;) a teacher of the Gentiles in faith and verity." Here, Paul is emphasizing that he was chosen by God to be a preacher of the Gospel, not by his own will but by divine appointment. To grasp the magnitude of this statement, we must dive deep into the role of a preacher in the New Testament and the emotional weight of Paul's calling. A preacher is more than just someone who stands before a crowd and speaks; a preacher is a messenger of hope, a vessel through which God's eternal truth flows, and one who proclaims the good news of Jesus Christ with a burning heart for the lost. Paul's life as a preacher was driven by one purpose: to make Christ known to all, to both Jew and Gentile, to the educated and the simple, to the rich and the poor, to everyone who would listen. This task was not easy, and it certainly wasn't glamorous. Paul didn't preach in air-conditioned churches with comfortable pews; no, he preached in synagogues where people sought to stone him, on the streets where crowds jeered, in prisons where he was shackled for his faith, and in foreign lands where his message was often met with hostility. And yet, Paul never faltered. He understood that the Gospel was the only message that could save souls, the only power strong enough to break the chains of sin, and the only truth worth giving his life for. His preaching was not just words; it was the outpouring of a heart consumed by the love of Christ. Every time Paul stood to preach, it was as if his soul was on fire, burning with the desire to see lives transformed by the power of the Gospel. He didn't preach to gain fame or applause; he preached because the message of Christ crucified was the most important message in the world. Imagine the emotional weight of carrying such a responsibility—the knowledge that eternity hung in the balance for those who heard him. Every sermon, every word that Paul spoke, was filled with passion, urgency, and deep

love for the lost. He preached because he knew what it was like to be lost. Before his conversion, Paul had been a zealous Pharisee, persecuting Christians and thinking he was doing God's will. But when he encountered the risen Christ on the road to Damascus, everything changed. He experienced firsthand the life-transforming power of the Gospel, and from that moment on, he was driven to share that same message with others. Paul's preaching wasn't just an intellectual exercise; it was personal. He had been saved by the very message he now preached, and he wanted nothing more than for others to experience the same grace and forgiveness he had received. But preaching the Gospel came with a cost. Paul was beaten, stoned, shipwrecked, imprisoned, and eventually martyred for the message he proclaimed. Yet, through all the suffering, Paul never regretted answering the call to be a preacher. In fact, he gloried in his sufferings, knowing that his trials were but a small price to pay for the privilege of proclaiming Christ. His preaching was not in vain. Everywhere Paul went, lives were changed. Entire cities were turned upside down as people responded to the Gospel and churches were planted. Paul's letters, written to these early churches, are filled with the same passion and urgency that marked his preaching. In his epistles, we see a man who cared deeply for the spiritual well-being of those he preached to. He didn't just preach and move on; he continued to shepherd these young believers, guiding them in their faith and encouraging them to stand firm in the truth. Paul's preaching was not limited by location or circumstance. Whether he was standing before a king or chained in a prison cell, he preached with the same fervor and conviction. He understood that the Gospel was not bound by human limitations; it was the power of God unto salvation for everyone who believed (Romans 1:16). And so, Paul preached, whether in freedom or in chains, whether to large crowds or to a single person. The message remained the same: Christ died for our sins, was buried, and rose again on the third day, and through faith in Him, we can be reconciled to God and receive eternal life. Paul's preaching was rooted in this simple yet profound truth, and it was this truth that had the power to change lives. As a preacher, Paul also knew that his words carried eternal significance. Every sermon, every conversation about the Gospel, was an opportunity for someone to come to know Christ. Paul lived with a sense of urgency because he knew that life was short, and eternity was long. He preached as if every moment was his last, not out of fear, but out of love for the lost. He didn't want anyone to miss out on the gift of salvation, and so he poured himself into his preaching, holding nothing back. Paul's life as a preacher is a testament to the transforming power of the Gospel. He was once an enemy of Christ, but through God's grace, he became one of the greatest preachers of the faith. His story reminds us that no one is too far gone for God to use. Paul's preaching wasn't polished or perfect by human standards, but it was powerful because it was anointed by the Holy Spirit. He relied not on his own strength or eloquence, but on the power of God to work through him. As he wrote in 1 Corinthians 2:4-5, "And my speech and my preaching was not with enticing words of man's wisdom, but in demonstration of the Spirit and of power: That your faith should not stand in the wisdom of men, but in the power of God." Paul's preaching was effective not because he was the most talented speaker, but because he was faithful to proclaim the truth of the Gospel and trusted God to do the rest. In the end, Paul's life as a preacher was marked by one thing: faithfulness. He was faithful to the call God had placed on his life, faithful to the message of the Gospel, and faithful to the people he ministered to. His reward was not in the applause of men, but in the knowledge that he had finished the race, kept the faith, and fulfilled his ministry (2 Timothy 4:7). Paul's legacy as a preacher of the Gospel lives on, inspiring generations of believers to take up the mantle of preaching Christ and Him crucified. His life reminds us that the Gospel is worth preaching, worth living for, and even worth dying for. As we look at Paul's example, we are challenged to live with the same passion and urgency, knowing that the message of the Gospel is the greatest message the world has ever known, and it is a message that must be preached to all people, in all places, at all times. Paul's life as a preacher of the Gospel is a testimony to the power of God's grace, the urgency of the Gospel, and the eternal significance of faithfully proclaiming Christ to a lost and dying world.

Chapter 3 - Servant of Jesus Christ

In Romans 1:1, the Apostle Paul begins his letter with these simple yet profound words: "Paul, a servant of Jesus Christ, called to be an apostle, separated unto the gospel of God." In these words, Paul identifies himself as a servant of Jesus Christ, and this title is one of the most powerful and humbling descriptions anyone can have. To be a servant of Jesus Christ means far more than just following Him—it means surrendering everything, laying down one's own life, plans, desires, and ambitions to take up the mission and purpose of Jesus. It means being completely devoted to His will, following Him wherever He leads, no matter the cost. Paul was not just a servant in name, but in every action, thought, and word, his entire life was centered around his devotion to Christ. This title captures the essence of Paul's identity; he lived and breathed his servanthood to Jesus. Imagine the depth of commitment it takes to become a servant in the truest sense—especially for someone like Paul, who once had status, power, and prestige as a Pharisee. Before his conversion, Paul had everything the world could offer: education, influence, and religious authority. But when he encountered Jesus on the road to Damascus, his life was radically transformed. In that moment, Paul realized that everything he had counted as gain was nothing compared to the surpassing worth of knowing Christ. His life became one of total service to the Lord, as he says in Philippians 3:8, "Yea doubtless, and I count all things but loss for the excellency of the knowledge of Christ Jesus my Lord." To be a servant of Christ was, for Paul, the highest honor and greatest privilege, even though it required the deepest sacrifice. Paul's servanthood to Jesus was not forced; it was a willing surrender, born out of love and gratitude for the incredible grace he had received. Paul knew that before he met Christ, he had been a slave to sin, lost in his own self-righteousness, blinded by his zeal for the law. But Christ freed him, gave him a new life, a new purpose, and a new identity. As Paul says in Galatians 2:20, "I am crucified with Christ:

nevertheless I live; yet not I, but Christ liveth in me." Paul's life as a servant of Christ was not about personal glory or recognition—it was about living in such a way that Christ would be glorified in everything he did. He didn't serve out of obligation or fear, but out of a deep love for his Savior who had given him everything. This was a love so strong that it compelled Paul to endure unimaginable hardships, to go to places no one else would go, to preach the Gospel to those who hated him, and to never give up, even when it meant facing beatings, imprisonment, shipwrecks, and eventually death. Being a servant of Jesus Christ meant living for something greater than himself, for a mission that transcended his own comfort or safety. In 2 Corinthians 11:23-28, Paul gives a glimpse into the trials he faced as a servant of Christ: "In labours more abundant, in stripes above measure, in prisons more frequent, in deaths oft." And yet, despite all of these hardships, Paul never complained, never wavered in his commitment, because he knew that his life belonged to Christ, and that serving Him was worth everything. For Paul, the title of servant wasn't one of weakness or lowliness in the way the world might think of it; rather, it was a badge of honor, because in serving Christ, he found true freedom, true joy, and true purpose. In a world where people seek status, power, and recognition, Paul shows us that the greatest calling is to be a servant of Jesus. Paul understood that to serve Christ was to follow in the footsteps of Jesus Himself, who came not to be served, but to serve and to give His life as a ransom for many (Mark 10:45). Paul modeled his life after his Savior, seeking not to exalt himself, but to exalt Christ in everything he did. He preached the Gospel tirelessly, traveled to far-off lands, endured rejection and persecution, all because he saw himself as a servant whose one mission was to make Jesus known. In 1 Corinthians 9:19, Paul says, "For though I be free from all men, yet have I made myself servant unto all, that I might gain the more." Paul's servanthood wasn't just about serving Jesus directly, but also about serving others in the name of Christ. He became all things to all people, whether Jew or Gentile, weak or strong, in order to win them to Christ. His heart was consumed with a love for people, because he knew that to serve Christ was also to serve those for whom Christ died. This is what it means to be a servant of Jesus Christ—to be so transformed by His love that you cannot help but pour that love out to others. Paul's servanthood also meant that he was not his own; he had been bought with a price, the precious blood of Jesus, and his life was no longer his to control. In 1 Corinthians 6:19-20, Paul reminds believers of this truth: "Ye are not your own... For ye are bought with a price: therefore glorify God in your body, and in your spirit, which are God's." Paul lived every day with this awareness that he was living for someone else, that his life was dedicated to the service of the One who had given His life for him. Paul's example teaches us that being a servant of Jesus Christ means total surrender—surrender of our will, our plans, our desires, our very lives. It means trusting that God's plan is far better than anything we could imagine for ourselves and that in serving Him, we find our true purpose. Paul's life as a servant of Christ wasn't easy, but it was full of joy, peace, and satisfaction, because he knew he was doing the will of God. Even when he was in prison, he could rejoice, as he wrote in Philippians 4:4, "Rejoice in the Lord alway: and again I say, Rejoice." Paul's joy came not from his circumstances, but from his relationship with Christ, from knowing that he was serving the King of kings. As a servant of Jesus, Paul found the deepest fulfillment, because he knew that his life had eternal significance. He wasn't living for temporary pleasures or fleeting rewards; he was living for the glory of God and the advancement of His Kingdom. Every hardship he endured, every sacrifice he made, was worth it, because he knew that his labor was not in vain in the Lord (1 Corinthians 15:58). Paul's life reminds us that being a servant of Jesus Christ is the greatest calling anyone can have. It's not about receiving praise or recognition from the world, but about living for the One who loved us and gave Himself for us. Paul's servanthood was marked by humility, by a deep sense of gratitude for the grace he had received, and by a burning desire to see others come to know the love of Christ. He didn't see himself as superior to anyone; in fact, he often referred to himself as the least of the apostles, not even worthy to be called an apostle because of his past persecution of the church (1 Corinthians 15:9). But it was this very humility that made Paul such a powerful servant of Christ, because he knew that everything he had, every gift, every success, was all by the grace of God. In 1 Corinthians 15:10, Paul writes, "But by the grace of God I am what I am: and his grace which was bestowed upon me was not in vain; but I laboured more abundantly than they all: yet not I, but the grace of God which was with me." Paul's life as a servant of Jesus Christ was a life of grace, a life transformed by the love and power of God. He knew that he could do nothing apart from Christ, but with Christ, all things were possible. And so he labored tirelessly, not in his own strength, but in the strength that God provided. As we look at Paul's life, we are reminded that being a servant of Jesus Christ is not about perfection; it's about faithfulness. It's about showing up, day after day, even when it's hard, even when the world is against you, even when you don't see the results you hoped for. It's about trusting that God is at work, even when we can't see it, and believing that He will accomplish His purposes through us if we remain faithful. Paul's servanthood was a life of faith, of trusting in the promises of God, of believing that the Gospel was worth giving everything for. In the end, Paul's life as a servant of Jesus Christ is an inspiration to us all. He shows us that true greatness is found not in seeking our own glory, but in laying down our lives for the sake of Christ and His Kingdom. He teaches us that the path of servanthood is not easy, but it is worth it, because in serving Christ, we find the true meaning of life. Paul's life challenges us to examine our own hearts: Are we living as servants of Jesus Christ? Are we willing to lay down our own plans and desires to follow Him? Are we willing to serve others in His name, even when it costs us? Paul's example calls us to a deeper level of surrender, a deeper commitment to the cause of Christ. And as we follow in his footsteps, we too can experience the joy, peace, and fulfillment that come from being a servant of the One who gave His life for us.

Chapter 4 - Ambassador in Bonds

In Ephesians 6:20, the Apostle Paul calls himself "an ambassador in bonds," and this phrase carries with it a depth of emotion, power, and inspiration that reflects Paul's entire life and ministry. To fully understand what it means to be an ambassador in bonds, we need to grasp the meaning of being an ambassador and the profound weight of being in bonds for Christ. An ambassador is someone who represents a higher authority, a messenger or diplomat sent by one kingdom or government to another. In this case, Paul was an ambassador for the greatest kingdom of all—the Kingdom of God. His mission was to proclaim the Gospel of Jesus Christ, to represent the values, the love, and the truth of God's Kingdom to a world lost in darkness. But unlike most ambassadors, Paul did not carry out his mission in the comfort and security of a royal court or embassy; instead, he was in bonds. He was in chains, imprisoned for the very message he had been sent to proclaim. Yet, Paul did not see his imprisonment as a limitation or a hindrance to his mission. Instead, he embraced his situation, knowing that even in chains, he was still a representative of Christ, still carrying out his divine calling. This is what makes his title "ambassador in bonds" so powerful and so deeply moving. Paul's chains were not a symbol of defeat; they were a badge of honor, a testimony to his unwavering commitment to Christ and the Gospel. Imagine the emotional weight of being in prison, surrounded by cold, iron bars, cut off from the outside world, yet still burning with the passion to share the message of salvation with all who would hear. Paul's physical freedom may have been taken from him, but his spirit remained free, filled with the love and power of Christ. His body was bound, but his heart was not, and his voice continued to speak the truth of the Gospel even from the depths of a prison cell. Being an ambassador in bonds means that no matter the circumstances, Paul remained faithful to his calling. He did not let his chains silence him or cause him to doubt his mission. In fact, Paul often spoke of his bonds as something to rejoice in. In Philippians 1:12-14, he writes, "But I would ye should understand, brethren, that the things which happened unto me have fallen out rather unto the furtherance of the gospel; So that my bonds in Christ are manifest in all the palace, and in all other places; And many of the brethren in the Lord, waxing confident by my bonds, are much more bold to speak the word without fear." Paul's imprisonment didn't stop the spread of the Gospel; it actually fueled it. His courage and faith in the face of suffering inspired others to preach with boldness, unafraid of the consequences. His chains became a platform from which the message of Christ reached even further. As an ambassador in bonds, Paul's mission was not just to proclaim the Gospel to the free, but also to those who were captive—both physically and spiritually. His chains connected him to a whole new audience: the soldiers who guarded him, the prisoners who were held alongside him, and even the officials who were responsible for his imprisonment. Paul took every opportunity, even in the most difficult of circumstances, to share the love of Christ. In Acts 16, we see an example of this when Paul and Silas, after being beaten and thrown into prison, began to sing praises to God in the middle of the night. Their faith and joy in the midst of suffering led to an earthquake that opened the prison doors, but even more importantly, it led to the conversion of the jailer and his entire household. This is what it means to be an ambassador in bonds—to represent Christ not just when things are easy, but in the darkest, most challenging moments of life. Paul's chains were a reminder that the Gospel is not bound by human limitations. The message of Jesus Christ cannot be silenced by prison walls or shackles. In 2 Timothy 2:9, Paul declares, "Wherein I suffer trouble, as an evil doer, even unto bonds; but the word of God is not bound." No matter where Paul was, no matter how tightly he was chained, the Word of God continued to spread, breaking through barriers, touching hearts, and changing lives. His role as an ambassador in bonds also reveals the deep sacrifice and commitment required to follow Christ. Paul knew that being a servant of Jesus would cost him everything—his freedom, his comfort, his reputation, and ultimately, his life. Yet, he considered it all worth it for the sake of knowing Christ and making Him known. In Philippians 3:8, he writes, "Yea doubtless, and I count all things but loss for the excellency of the knowledge of Christ Jesus my Lord: for whom I have suffered the loss of all things, and do count them but dung, that I may win Christ." Paul's willingness to suffer, to endure chains and imprisonment, was a testament to the incomparable value of Christ. He knew that nothing in this world could compare to the joy and fulfillment of being in relationship with Jesus and serving Him. His chains were not a burden; they were a privilege, a reflection of the great love he had for His Savior. Paul's example as an ambassador in bonds challenges us to examine our own lives and our own commitment to Christ. Are we willing to serve Jesus no matter the cost? Are we willing to represent Him even when it means facing hardship, rejection, or suffering? Paul's life shows us that true service to Christ requires sacrifice, but it also brings with it the deepest joy and the greatest purpose. As Paul sat in chains, he could have easily given in to despair. He could have questioned why God allowed him to suffer, why he was imprisoned when he had been so faithful to preach the Gospel. But instead, Paul chose to see his chains as an opportunity. He understood that his suffering had a purpose, that God was using his imprisonment to advance the Gospel in ways that he couldn't even imagine. In Romans 8:28, Paul famously writes, "And we know that all things work together for good to them that love God, to them who are the called according to his purpose." Paul believed this with all his heart, and his life reflected that belief. He trusted that even in the darkest moments, God was at work, using his suffering to bring about something greater. His faith in God's plan, even when he couldn't see it, is a powerful example to us all. Another important aspect of Paul's role as an ambassador in bonds is the way he continued to encourage and build up the church, even from prison. Many of Paul's letters, known as the "Prison Epistles," were written while he was in chains. These letters—Ephesians, Philippians, Colossians, and Philemon—are filled with wisdom, encouragement, and love for the believers. Paul didn't let his own suffering stop him from ministering to others. He didn't focus on his own pain or hardship; instead, he poured out his heart to strengthen and uplift the church. In Ephesians 6:18-20, right before he calls himself an ambassador in bonds, Paul urges the believers to pray for him, not that he would be released from prison, but that he would be bold in proclaiming the Gospel: "Praying always with all prayer and supplication in the Spirit... And for me, that utterance may be given unto me, that I may open my mouth boldly, to make known the mystery of the gospel." Even in chains, Paul's greatest concern was not for his own comfort or safety, but for the Gospel to be preached with boldness and clarity. His heart was so fully devoted to Christ that nothing else mattered. He was willing to endure any hardship if it meant that more people would hear the message of salvation. Paul's life as an ambassador in bonds is a beautiful example of what it means to be fully surrendered to Christ. His chains, which the world might have seen as a sign of defeat, were actually a testament to his victory in Christ. Paul understood that true freedom is not found in physical liberty, but in spiritual liberation through Jesus. He knew that no matter what happened to his body, his soul was secure in Christ, and that gave him the strength to endure anything. In 2 Corinthians 4:8-9, Paul writes, "We are troubled on every side, yet not distressed; we are perplexed, but not in despair; Persecuted, but not forsaken; cast down, but not destroyed." These words reflect the unshakable faith and resilience that defined Paul's life as an ambassador in bonds. He was pressed, but not crushed; he was persecuted, but not abandoned. His hope was firmly anchored in Christ, and that hope gave him the courage to keep going, even when everything seemed to be against him. As an ambassador in bonds, Paul's life was a living testimony to the power of the Gospel. His chains didn't limit him; they magnified his witness. They showed the world that the message of Christ is worth everything, that it is a message so powerful that even imprisonment and suffering cannot silence it. Paul's chains were a reminder that the Gospel is not just for the good times, but for the hard times as well. It is a message of hope, not just for those who are free, but for those who are in bondage—whether physical, emotional, or spiritual. Paul's life challenges us to ask ourselves: What are we willing to endure for the sake of the Gospel? Are we willing to be ambassadors for Christ, even if it means facing hardship or persecution? Paul's example calls us to a deeper level of commitment, a willingness to serve Christ no matter the cost. His life reminds us that true freedom is found not in avoiding suffering, but in embracing our calling, even when it leads us into difficult places. Paul's role as an ambassador in bonds is an inspiring and powerful example of what it means to live fully for Christ. His life was marked by sacrifice, by unwavering faith, and by a deep love for the Gospel. He showed us that even in the darkest of circumstances, we can still represent Christ with boldness and joy. His chains, rather than being a symbol of defeat, became a testimony to the unstoppable power of the Gospel and the faithfulness of God. Paul's life as an ambassador in bonds continues to inspire and challenge believers today, calling us to live with the same passion, dedication, and trust in the God who is with us in every trial, in every situation, and in every moment.

Chapter 5 - Minister of the New Covenant

In 2 Corinthians 3:6, Paul writes, "Who also hath made us able ministers of the new testament; not of the letter, but of the spirit: for the letter killeth, but the spirit giveth life." Here, Paul identifies himself as a minister of the New Covenant, a title that holds a depth of meaning and a weight of responsibility beyond anything this world could offer. To understand the significance of being a minister of the New Covenant, we first have to grasp the contrast between the Old Covenant and the New Covenant. The Old Covenant, given to Moses on Mount Sinai, was a covenant of law—rules written on stone tablets, a covenant of rituals, sacrifices, and commandments that pointed toward God's holiness but could never make anyone righteous. Under the Old Covenant, people were bound by the letter of the law, and though the law was good, it also revealed humanity's inability to keep it perfectly. It showed the holiness of God and the sinfulness of man, leaving us aware of our failures and in desperate need of a Savior. But then, Jesus came. His life, death, and resurrection ushered in a New Covenant, a covenant not written on tablets of stone but written on the hearts of men and women through the Holy Spirit. The New Covenant is not about external rituals or keeping a set of laws; it's about an internal transformation, a new birth, a relationship with God that is based on grace, not works, on the Spirit, not the letter. Paul, as a minister of this New Covenant, was called to proclaim the greatest message ever given to mankind—that through Jesus Christ, sinners can be forgiven, hearts can be made new, and eternal life can be received, not through our own efforts but through faith in the finished work of Christ. Imagine the power of that message, the hope it brings to the broken, the freedom it gives to those trapped in the chains of sin and shame. Paul's role as a minister of the New Covenant was to share this message of hope and transformation, to bring life where there had only been death, to declare that in Christ, the old has passed away, and all things have become new (2 Corinthians

5:17). This was not just a message of forgiveness for sins but of total and complete renewal, the promise that the Spirit of God would dwell in every believer, empowering them to live a life of victory and freedom in Christ. Paul was not just delivering information; he was proclaiming a message that had the power to change lives from the inside out. Being a minister of the New Covenant meant that Paul was not just teaching rules or doctrines; he was a vessel through which the very power of God's Spirit flowed. He was bringing the light of the Gospel to a world lost in darkness, and through the Spirit, that light was transforming hearts. Paul contrasts the Old Covenant, which he says "killeth," with the New Covenant, which "giveth life." Under the Old Covenant, no matter how hard people tried, they could never fully live up to the demands of the law. The law showed them their sin, but it didn't give them the power to overcome it. But under the New Covenant, through the Holy Spirit, believers are given the power to live a new life in Christ. They are no longer slaves to sin but are made alive in Christ, free to walk in the Spirit and live in a way that pleases God. As a minister of the New Covenant, Paul was sent to proclaim this glorious truth, that in Christ, we are no longer condemned by the law but are set free by the Spirit of life. Imagine the weight of this responsibility, the joy of sharing such good news with people who had lived their whole lives under the burden of trying to earn their way to God. Paul's message was revolutionary. It was liberating. It was the fulfillment of the promises that the prophets had spoken of for centuries—that God would make a new covenant with His people, one in which He would "put my law in their inward parts, and write it in their hearts" (Jeremiah 31:33). Paul was the one chosen by God to bring this message to the Gentiles, to those who had been far from God, to tell them that through Christ, they too were included in this New Covenant, that they too could receive the Spirit and be part of God's family. Paul's life as a minister of the New Covenant was not without its challenges. He faced intense opposition, persecution, and hardship. He was beaten, imprisoned, shipwrecked, and ultimately martyred for the message he preached. But Paul considered all of these sufferings to be worth it because he knew the power of the Gospel he was entrusted to share. In Romans 1:16, Paul boldly declares, "For I am not ashamed of the gospel of Christ: for it is the power of God unto salvation to every one that believeth." Paul's confidence in the message of the New Covenant wasn't based on human wisdom or persuasion; it was rooted in the reality that the Gospel is the very power of God at work in the world, transforming lives, setting captives free, and bringing people into a right relationship with God. Paul's role as a minister of the New Covenant was deeply personal for him. He knew what it was like to be lost in sin and self-righteousness. Before his conversion, Paul had been a zealous Pharisee, deeply committed to the law and to persecuting Christians. But when he encountered the risen Christ on the road to Damascus, his life was forever changed. He experienced firsthand the grace and mercy of God, the forgiveness of sins, and the new life that comes through faith in Jesus. Paul never forgot the grace he had received, and it fueled his passion to share that grace with others. He understood that the New Covenant was not just a theological concept; it was a living reality that had transformed his own heart and life. He had been a recipient of the grace of God, and now he was called to be a minister of that grace to others. This is what drove Paul to preach the Gospel with such urgency and passion. He knew that the message of the New Covenant was the only hope for a world trapped in sin and death. As a minister of the New Covenant, Paul was not offering people more rules to follow or a new set of religious practices. He was offering them a relationship with the living God, a relationship made possible through the sacrifice of Jesus on the cross. Paul's message was one of reconciliation—that through Christ, God was reconciling the world to Himself, not counting their sins against them (2 Corinthians 5:19). This message of reconciliation is at the heart of the New Covenant. It's the promise that, because of Jesus, we can have peace with God, our sins forgiven, and our hearts made new. Paul's role as a minister of the New Covenant was to be a messenger of this reconciliation, to tell people that no matter how far they had strayed, no matter how great their sin, they could be brought back into fellowship with God through faith in Jesus. And this wasn't just a message for the Jews; it was a message for all people, Jew and Gentile alike. Paul was called to be the apostle to the Gentiles, to bring the message of the New Covenant to those who had been outside the covenant promises of Israel. Through Christ, the barriers between Jew and Gentile were torn down, and all people were invited to come into the family of God. As a minister of the New Covenant, Paul was entrusted with this message of radical inclusion—that in Christ, "there is neither Jew nor Greek, there is neither bond nor free, there is neither male nor female: for ye are all one in Christ Jesus" (Galatians 3:28). This was a message that shook the foundations of the religious and social structures of Paul's day, but it was also a message of incredible hope and freedom. Paul's life as a minister of the New Covenant was marked by the power of the Holy Spirit. He wasn't just preaching words; he was ministering in the power of the Spirit, and that made all the difference. In 1 Corinthians 2:4-5, Paul says, "And my speech and my preaching was not with enticing words of man's wisdom, but in demonstration of the Spirit and of power: That your faith should not stand in the wisdom of men, but in the power of God." Paul knew that it wasn't his eloquence or intelligence that would change hearts; it was the Spirit of God working through him. As a minister of the New Covenant, Paul relied completely on the Spirit to do the work of transformation in people's lives. He wasn't trying to convince people to follow a new set of rules; he was pointing them to Jesus, the One who could give them a new heart and fill them with the Holy Spirit. The Spirit was the key to the New Covenant. Under the Old Covenant, people had the law, but they didn't have the power to keep it. But under the New Covenant, God gives us His Spirit, who empowers us to live the life we were created to live. Paul's role as a minister of the New Covenant was to lead people into that life, to show them that in Christ, they were no longer slaves to sin but were free to live in the power of the Spirit. In Romans 8:1-2, Paul writes, "There is therefore now no condemnation to them which are in Christ Jesus, who walk not after the flesh, but after the Spirit. For the law of the Spirit of life in Christ Jesus hath made me free from the law of sin and death." This is the heart of the New Covenant—that through the Spirit, we are set free from the power of sin and death and given new life in Christ. As a minister of the New Covenant, Paul's life was a testimony to the transforming power of that new life. He had been a persecutor of the church, but through the grace of God, he became one of its greatest leaders and evangelists. His story is a powerful reminder that no one is beyond the reach of God's grace, that through the New Covenant, anyone can be made new. Paul's life as a minister of the New Covenant was one of total surrender to Christ. He gave everything for the sake of the Gospel, enduring persecution, hardship, and suffering so that others could hear the message of the New Covenant and experience the same life-changing power that he had experienced. In Philippians 3:7-8, Paul writes, "But what things were gain to me, those I counted loss for Christ. Yea doubtless, and I count all things but loss for the excellency of the knowledge of Christ Jesus my Lord: for whom I have suffered the loss of all things, and do count them but dung, that I may win Christ." Paul's life as a minister of the New Covenant was one of total dedication to Christ and His mission. He was willing to suffer, to sacrifice, and to lay down his life because he knew the surpassing worth of knowing Christ and making Him known. As a minister of the New Covenant, Paul's life continues to inspire and challenge us today. His message is still the same—that through Christ, we can be reconciled to God, made new by the Spirit, and set free to live the life God created us to live. Paul's role as a minister of the New Covenant was not just a title; it was a calling that defined his entire life. And as we look at his example, we are reminded of the power of the Gospel, the power of the New Covenant, and the incredible grace of God that can transform any heart and life.

Chapter 6 - Chosen Vessel of Christ

In Acts 9:15, the Lord says of Paul, "Go thy way: for he is a chosen vessel unto me, to bear my name before the Gentiles, and kings, and the children of Israel." This simple yet powerful statement reveals a truth about the incredible calling on Paul's life, and it speaks to the heart of what it means to be a chosen vessel of Christ. A vessel is something that carries and contains, something that is filled with a purpose greater than itself. For Paul, being a chosen vessel meant that he was handpicked by God Himself, set apart for a mission so significant, so transformative, that it would change the course of history. This calling wasn't based on Paul's qualifications or worthiness—far from it. Before his conversion, Paul, known as Saul, was a zealous Pharisee, full of hatred for the followers of Jesus. He was a persecutor of the church, determined to destroy what he saw as a dangerous movement. But God, in His infinite mercy and grace, looked past Saul's hatred and saw something else: He saw a man who, when transformed by the power of Christ, could be used in a mighty way to spread the Gospel. When God chooses someone, it's not because of who they are, but because of what He can do through them. This is the beauty of Paul's story. He was not chosen because he was already good, already righteous, or already qualified. He was chosen because God, in His wisdom, saw the potential for transformation, for redemption, and for a life that could be used to glorify Him. God's choosing of Paul was an act of grace, a divine appointment that would take a man from darkness into light, from being a persecutor of Christians to being one of the greatest missionaries and apostles the world has ever known. Imagine the emotional weight of that calling. Paul was chosen not just to follow Jesus but to bear His name before the Gentiles, the kings, and the children of Israel. This was a mission that would require him to go to the ends of the earth, to preach the Gospel in the face of persecution, to stand before rulers and authorities who would often reject his message, and to endure suffering, hardship, and imprisonment. Yet Paul embraced his calling with everything he had, because he understood that being a chosen vessel of Christ meant that his life no longer belonged to him. From the moment Paul encountered Jesus on the road to Damascus, his life was forever changed. In that moment, he went from being Saul, the persecutor, to Paul, the chosen vessel. The same man who once sought to destroy the church now became one of its greatest builders. The same man who once hated the name of Jesus now bore that name with pride, carrying it to the far reaches of the Roman Empire, proclaiming it to both Jew and Gentile alike. Paul's life as a chosen vessel of Christ was marked by a deep sense of purpose, a burning passion to fulfill the mission God had given him. He knew that he had been chosen for a reason, that his life had a divine purpose, and that every moment, every step he took, was part of a larger plan. Paul's calling as a chosen vessel didn't mean that his life would be easy. In fact, it meant the opposite. From the moment he began his ministry, Paul faced intense opposition, persecution, and suffering. He was beaten, stoned, imprisoned, shipwrecked, and eventually martyred for his faith. But through it all, Paul never wavered, because he knew that his life was not his own. He had been chosen by God, and that calling gave him the strength to endure even the most difficult trials. As a chosen vessel of Christ, Paul's life became a living sacrifice, poured out for the sake of the Gospel. In Philippians 1:21, Paul famously writes, "For to me to live is Christ, and to die is gain." This was the heart of Paul's life as a chosen vessel. He understood that his life was no longer about his own desires, ambitions, or plans. It was about Christ—living for Him, serving Him, and making Him known to the world. Paul's calling as a chosen vessel was not just about preaching the Gospel; it was about embodying it. His entire life was a testimony to the transformative power of Christ. He didn't just speak about the grace of God; he lived it. He didn't just talk about the love of Jesus; he showed it in the way he treated others, the way he ministered to both Jews and Gentiles, the way he risked his own life to bring the message of salvation to those who had never heard it. Paul's life as a chosen vessel is a powerful reminder that when God chooses us, it's not because of anything we have done, but because of His grace. Paul didn't deserve to be chosen—none of us do. But God, in His mercy, calls us, not because we are worthy, but because He loves us and has a purpose for our lives. Paul's story reminds us that no one is beyond the reach of God's grace. If God could choose Paul, a man who had once been an enemy of the church, to be His chosen vessel, then He can choose any of us. No matter where we've been, no matter what we've done, God can transform our lives and use us for His glory. Being a chosen vessel of Christ also means that we are filled with His Spirit, empowered to do the work He has called us to do. Paul wasn't chosen and then left to figure it out on his own. He was filled with the Holy Spirit, who gave him the strength, wisdom, and courage to fulfill his mission. In 2 Corinthians 12:9, Paul writes, "And he said unto me, My grace is sufficient for thee: for my strength is made perfect in weakness." Paul knew that it wasn't his own strength that sustained him, but the strength of Christ working through him. As a chosen vessel, Paul was dependent on the power of the Holy Spirit to accomplish the work God had given him. He wasn't relying on his own abilities or qualifications; he was relying on the grace of God. This is what it means to be a chosen vessel of Christ—not that we are perfect or capable in ourselves, but that we are willing to be used by God, trusting in His strength to carry us through. Paul's life as a chosen vessel of Christ is a story of redemption, transformation, and purpose. It's a story that reminds us that God doesn't choose us because we are already qualified, but because He sees what we can become through His grace. Paul's life challenges us to ask ourselves: Are we willing to be chosen vessels of Christ? Are we willing to lay down our own lives, our own plans, and our own desires to be used by Him for His glory? Paul's example shows us that the life of a chosen vessel is not easy, but it is full of meaning, purpose, and the deep joy that comes from knowing we are serving the King of kings. As a chosen vessel, Paul's life was also marked by a deep sense of responsibility. He knew that he had been entrusted with the greatest message the world had ever known—the message of the Gospel. In 1 Corinthians 9:16, Paul writes, "For though I preach the gospel, I have nothing to glory of: for necessity is laid upon me; yea, woe is unto me, if I preach not the gospel!" Paul felt the weight of his calling as a chosen vessel. He knew that he had been chosen for a purpose, and that purpose was to share the Gospel with as many people as possible. Paul's sense of urgency in fulfilling his calling is something that should inspire and challenge us. As chosen vessels of Christ, we too have been entrusted with the message of the Gospel. We have been chosen to bear His name, to share His love with the world, to be His hands and feet in a world that desperately needs Him. Paul's life reminds us that this calling is not something to be taken lightly. It is a privilege, an honor, and a responsibility. Paul's role as a chosen vessel of Christ also speaks to the idea of being set apart. When God chose Paul, He set him apart for a specific purpose. Paul wasn't called to blend in with the world; he was called to stand out, to be different, to be a light in the darkness. As chosen vessels of Christ, we are also called to be set apart. In Romans 12:2, Paul writes, "And be not conformed to this world: but be ye transformed by the renewing of your mind, that ye may prove what is that good, and acceptable, and perfect, will of God." Being a chosen vessel means that we are called to live differently, to live in a way that reflects the love, grace, and truth of Jesus. Paul's life as a chosen vessel was one of total devotion to Christ. He wasn't half-hearted in his commitment; he was all in. He gave everything he had—his time, his energy, his resources, even his life—for the sake of the Gospel. In 2 Timothy 4:7, as Paul neared the end of his life, he wrote, "I have fought a good fight, I have finished my course, I have kept the faith." Paul's life as a chosen vessel was one of perseverance, faithfulness, and unwavering commitment to the mission God had given him. He didn't give up when things got hard; he pressed on, knowing that his reward was not in this life, but in the life to come. Paul's story as a chosen vessel of Christ is a story that continues to inspire and challenge believers today. It's a story of how God can take the most unlikely of people, transform their lives, and use them in ways they never could have imagined. It's a story of grace, of redemption, and of the incredible power of the Gospel. Paul's life reminds us that when God chooses us, it's not because of who we are, but because of who He is. It's a reminder that God's grace is greater than our past, that His strength is made perfect in our weakness, and that when we surrender our lives to Him, He can use us for His glory in ways we never thought possible. As a chosen vessel of Christ, Paul's life was a living testimony to the power of God's grace. He was a man who had once been lost, but through Christ, he was found. He was a man who had once been blind, but through Christ, his eyes were opened. He was a man who had once been a persecutor of the church, but through Christ, he became one of its greatest champions. Paul's life as a chosen vessel of Christ is a powerful reminder that no one is beyond the reach of God's grace, and that when we are chosen by Him, our lives can be used to make an eternal impact for His kingdom.

Chapter 7 - Defender of the Faith

In Philippians 1:7, the Apostle Paul speaks with deep affection to the believers in Philippi, saying, "Even as it is meet for me to think this of you all, because I have you in my heart; inasmuch as both in my bonds, and in the defence and confirmation of the gospel, ye all are partakers of my grace." This verse gives us a glimpse into Paul's role as a "defender of the faith," a title that carries with it immense responsibility, courage, and devotion. Paul was not only a preacher of the Gospel, but he stood boldly as a defender of the very faith he proclaimed. In every aspect of his life—from his preaching to his suffering, from his chains to his writings—Paul was engaged in a spiritual battle to protect and proclaim the truth of the Gospel. To defend the faith means to stand firm against opposition, to hold fast to the truth of God's Word when others seek to distort it, and to be unshaken by the pressures and persecutions that try to silence the message of Christ. Paul's defense of the faith was not merely intellectual; it was deeply personal and emotional. He had been radically transformed by his encounter with Jesus on the road to Damascus, and from that moment forward, his entire life was dedicated to defending the truth of the Gospel. He knew firsthand the power of God's grace, and he was willing to suffer anything to ensure that others could come to know that same grace. Paul's defense of the faith came with great cost. He was beaten, stoned, imprisoned, shipwrecked, and eventually martyred for the message he defended. But through it all, he remained steadfast, not because of his own strength, but because of the unshakable faith he had in the truth of the Gospel and the faithfulness of God. As a defender of the faith, Paul understood that the Gospel was not just a set of beliefs or doctrines; it was the power of God unto salvation for everyone who believes (Romans 1:16). This was a truth worth defending at all costs. It was a truth that set people free from the bondage of sin and death, and Paul was determined to defend it with every breath he had. In Philippians 1:7, Paul mentions his bonds, which remind us that even while he was physically chained, his spirit remained free, and his defense of the faith continued. Paul's imprisonment did not hinder the Gospel; instead, it became a platform for him to further defend the faith. His chains were a testament to his unwavering commitment to Christ, and they became an encouragement to the believers, showing them that the Gospel was worth defending, even if it meant suffering. Paul's life as a defender of the faith was also marked by a deep love for the church. He didn't defend the faith out of pride or a desire to win arguments; he defended it because he loved God, and he loved people. He knew that the truth of the Gospel was the only hope for a lost and dying world, and he was willing to lay down his life to ensure that others could hear and believe. Paul's love for the Philippians, expressed in Philippians 1:7, shows us that defending the faith is not just about standing against opposition; it's about standing for something—for the salvation of souls, for the truth of God's Word, for the hope that only Jesus can bring. Paul was a defender of the faith because he believed with all his heart that Jesus was the way, the truth, and the life, and he knew that no one could come to the Father except through Him (John 14:6). This was the truth that Paul gave his life to defend. Paul's defense of the faith also involved confirming the truth of the Gospel. In Philippians 1:7, he speaks of both defending and confirming the Gospel, showing us that his role was not just to argue against false teachings, but to affirm the truth of God's Word, to build up the church in their faith, and to help them grow in their understanding of the Gospel. Paul was a teacher, a shepherd, and a spiritual father to many, and his defense of the faith was always done with the goal of edifying the church and strengthening believers in their walk with Christ. Paul's letters, which make up a large portion of the New Testament, are filled with his defense of the faith. He addressed false teachings, corrected errors, and clarified the truth of the Gospel, always pointing people back to Jesus and the message of salvation by grace through faith. His writings continue to serve as a defense of the faith for us today, guiding us in truth and helping us to stand firm in our own faith. As a defender of the faith, Paul was also keenly aware of the spiritual battle that was taking place. He knew that defending the faith wasn't just about debating ideas or refuting false teachings; it was about standing against the forces of darkness that sought to blind people to the truth of the Gospel. In Ephesians 6:12, Paul writes, "For we wrestle not against flesh and blood, but against principalities, against powers, against the rulers of the darkness of this world, against spiritual wickedness in high places." Paul's defense of the faith was spiritual warfare, and he knew that he could not fight this battle in his own strength. He relied completely on the power of the Holy Spirit to give him the wisdom, courage, and strength he needed to stand firm in the face of opposition. Paul's life as a defender of the faith challenges us to examine our own commitment to the Gospel. Are we willing to stand firm in our faith, even when it costs us? Are we willing to defend the truth of God's Word, even when it's unpopular or met with resistance? Paul's example shows us that defending the faith is not optional for the believer; it is part of our calling as followers of Christ. We are called to be defenders of the faith in our own lives, to stand up for the truth of the Gospel, and to share the message of salvation with those around us. Paul's life also reminds us that defending the faith is not just about words; it's about how we live. Paul didn't just preach the Gospel; he lived it. His life was a testimony to the power of the Gospel, and his willingness to suffer for the faith showed the depth of his commitment to Christ. As defenders of the faith, we are called to live in such a way that our lives reflect the truth of the Gospel. Our words must be backed up by our actions, and our love for God and for others must be evident in everything we do. Paul's role as a defender of the faith also involved great humility. He didn't defend the faith to make a name for himself or to prove that he was right; he did it out of obedience to God and a desire to see others come to know the truth. In Philippians 1:7, we see Paul's deep love and humility as he speaks of the Philippians as "partakers of my grace." Paul knew that everything he had, including his ability to defend the faith, was a result of God's grace. He didn't boast in his own strength or wisdom; he boasted in the Lord and gave all the glory to God. As defenders of the faith, we must follow Paul's example of humility, recognizing that it is only by God's grace that we can stand firm in our faith and share the Gospel with others. Paul's defense of the faith was not about winning arguments or being right; it was about winning souls for Christ. He understood that the Gospel was the only hope for a world lost in sin, and he was willing to do whatever it took to share that message with as many people as possible. In 1 Corinthians 9:22, Paul writes, "I am made all things to all men, that I might by all means save some." Paul's defense of the faith was motivated by love—love for God and love for people. He wanted everyone to know the truth of the Gospel, and he was willing to endure any hardship, any persecution, any trial, to make that happen. Paul's life as a defender of the faith was a life of sacrifice. He gave up his own comfort, his own safety, and ultimately his own life for the sake of the Gospel. In 2 Timothy 4:7, as Paul neared the end of his life, he wrote, "I have fought a good fight, I have finished my course, I have kept the faith." Paul's defense of the faith was not just a momentary decision; it was a lifelong commitment. He fought the good fight, and he finished the race, holding fast to the faith he had been given. His life is a powerful reminder that defending the faith is not just about a single moment of courage, but about a lifetime of faithfulness to Christ. As we reflect on Paul's role as a defender of the faith, we are challenged to follow in his footsteps. We may not face the same kind of persecution that Paul did, but we are still called to stand firm in our faith, to proclaim the truth of the Gospel, and to defend it against the lies and deceptions of the world. We are called to live lives that reflect the love, grace, and truth of Jesus, and to share that message with those around us, even when it's difficult or unpopular. Paul's life as a defender of the faith inspires us to be bold in our witness, steadfast in our commitment to Christ, and faithful in our calling as followers of Jesus. His example reminds us that defending the faith is not about our own strength or abilities, but about relying on the power of God to work through us. Just as Paul relied on the Holy Spirit to guide and strengthen him in his defense of the faith, we too must depend on the Spirit to equip us for the task. Paul's life shows us that defending the faith is not just about standing against opposition, but about standing for the truth of the Gospel with love, humility, and grace. His legacy as a defender of the faith continues to inspire and challenge us today, calling us to live lives that honor Christ and to boldly proclaim the message of salvation to a world in desperate need of hope. As we look at Paul's life, we are reminded that defending the faith is not just about words, but about a life fully surrendered to Christ, a life that reflects the truth of the Gospel in everything we say and do. Paul's role as a defender of the faith is a powerful example of what it means to live for Christ, to stand firm in the truth, and to proclaim the Gospel with boldness, no matter the cost. His life challenges us to be defenders of the faith in our own lives, to stand up for the truth of God's Word, and to share the message of Jesus with those around us, knowing that the Gospel is the power of God unto salvation for everyone who believes.

Chapter 8 - Teacher of the Gentiles

In 2 Timothy 1:11, Paul writes, "Whereunto I am appointed a preacher, and an apostle, and a teacher of the Gentiles." This simple yet powerful statement reveals a deep and emotional truth about Paul's calling and the heart of his ministry. To be a "teacher of the Gentiles" was not merely a role Paul took on, but it was a divine appointment, a mission that consumed his entire life with purpose and passion. Paul, a former Pharisee, who once zealously persecuted Christians, was transformed by the grace of Jesus Christ, and through that transformation, God gave him the incredible responsibility to teach the Gentiles—the non-Jewish people of the world—about the Gospel of Jesus Christ. For centuries, the Jewish people had been seen as the chosen nation, the ones who were given the law of God through Moses, the ones through whom the Messiah would come. The Gentiles, on the other hand, were often viewed as outsiders, separated from the promises of God. But when Jesus died and rose again, He tore down the wall of division, opening the way for all people—Jew and Gentile alike—to be reconciled to God through faith in Him. And it was Paul's unique mission to teach this truth, to show the Gentiles that they were no longer strangers to the covenants of promise but were now fellow heirs with the Jews in Christ. Imagine the emotional and spiritual weight of that calling—to be the one tasked with bringing the light of the Gospel to those who had been living in darkness for so long, to be the bridge that connected those who were far off with the God who loved them. Paul understood that his role as a teacher of the Gentiles was not just about imparting knowledge or teaching doctrines; it was about leading people into a transformative relationship with Jesus Christ, one that would change their lives forever. His heart was filled with a burning passion to see the Gentiles come to know the saving grace of God, and he devoted every part of himself to that mission, even when it meant facing hardship, persecution, and rejection. Being a teacher of

the Gentiles required Paul to step outside of his own cultural and religious background and to embrace a new way of thinking, a new way of living. It required humility, compassion, and an open heart. Paul had to lay aside his former prejudices, his former pride in his Jewish heritage, and recognize that the love of God extended beyond the borders of Israel, that it reached into every nation, every tribe, every people. Paul's teaching wasn't just about explaining the Gospel; it was about embodying the Gospel, showing the Gentiles through his words and his actions that they were loved by God, that they were valuable in His eyes, and that they too had a place in His kingdom. Paul's role as a teacher of the Gentiles was one of great joy but also great sacrifice. He traveled tirelessly across the Roman Empire, preaching in synagogues, marketplaces, homes, and public squares, often facing resistance, hostility, and even physical violence. But Paul never gave up because he knew that the message he carried was worth everything. He was compelled by the love of Christ to keep going, to keep teaching, to keep reaching out to those who had never heard the Gospel. In Romans 10:14-15, Paul writes, "How then shall they call on him in whom they have not believed? and how shall they believe in him of whom they have not heard? and how shall they hear without a preacher? And how shall they preach, except they be sent?" Paul knew that he had been sent by God to bring the message of salvation to the Gentiles, and he was determined to fulfill that calling no matter the cost. Paul's teaching was not just about words; it was about the power of the Holy Spirit working through him to change lives. He wasn't simply giving lectures or sermons; he was preaching with power, with conviction, with anointing. In 1 Corinthians 2:4-5, Paul writes, "And my speech and my preaching was not with enticing words of man's wisdom, but in demonstration of the Spirit and of power: That your faith should not stand in the wisdom of men, but in the power of God." Paul understood that true teaching wasn't about eloquence or persuasion; it was about allowing the Spirit of God to move through him and touch the hearts of those who listened. As a teacher of the Gentiles, Paul was more than a preacher; he was a shepherd, a mentor, a spiritual father. He cared deeply for the people he ministered to, often referring to them as his spiritual children. In 1 Thessalonians 2:7-8, he writes, "But we were gentle among you, even as a nurse cherisheth her children: So being affectionately desirous of you, we were willing to have imparted unto you, not the gospel of

God only, but also our own souls, because ye were dear unto us." Paul wasn't just concerned with their salvation; he was invested in their spiritual growth, their well-being, their journey of faith. His letters to the churches he planted are filled with encouragement, correction, instruction, and love. He poured out his heart to them, guiding them in their new faith, helping them navigate the challenges of living for Christ in a world that often opposed them. Paul's role as a teacher of the Gentiles also involved breaking down barriers. The early church was made up of people from different backgrounds—Jews and Gentiles, slaves and free, men and women—and these groups often had deep divisions and misunderstandings. But Paul was committed to teaching them that in Christ, those divisions no longer mattered. In Galatians 3:28, he writes, "There is neither Jew nor Greek, there is neither bond nor free, there is neither male nor female: for ye are all one in Christ Jesus." Paul's teaching emphasized the unity of the body of Christ, the truth that all believers, regardless of their background, were equal and united in their faith. This was a radical message for his time, but it was at the heart of the Gospel, and Paul was relentless in teaching it. As a teacher of the Gentiles, Paul faced many challenges, including opposition from his own people, the Jews, who struggled to accept that the Gentiles could be included in God's plan of salvation without first becoming Jewish. Paul had to defend the truth of the Gospel, not only to the Gentiles but also to his fellow Jews. In Acts 15, we see Paul standing up at the Jerusalem Council, arguing passionately that Gentile believers should not be required to follow the Jewish law in order to be saved, because salvation comes through faith in Jesus Christ alone. Paul's defense of the Gospel was not just a matter of theological debate; it was a matter of life and death for the Gentiles, who were being told that they couldn't fully belong to the family of God unless they followed certain rules and rituals. Paul knew that the Gospel was a message of grace, not works, and he fought tirelessly to ensure that the Gentiles understood that their acceptance by God was based on faith in Christ, not on their ability to keep the law. This was the heart of Paul's teaching—that in Christ, the old distinctions no longer applied, and everyone, regardless of their background, could come to God through faith in Jesus. Paul's life as a teacher of the Gentiles was a life of constant service and sacrifice. He traveled far and wide, often at great personal cost, to make sure that the Gentiles heard the message of salvation. He endured shipwrecks, beatings, imprisonment, and hunger, but he counted it all joy because he knew that his suffering was not in vain. In Philippians 3:8, Paul writes, "Yea doubtless, and I count all things but loss for the excellency of the knowledge of Christ Jesus my Lord: for whom I have suffered the loss of all things, and do count them but dung, that I may win Christ." Paul's life as a teacher of the Gentiles was driven by a deep, unshakable love for Christ and for the people he was called to serve. He saw himself not as someone seeking glory or recognition, but as a servant of Christ, appointed to bring the good news to those who had never heard it before. His heart was burdened for the Gentiles, and he was willing to endure anything to see them come to faith in Jesus. Paul's example as a teacher of the Gentiles challenges us today. It reminds us that the call to teach and share the Gospel is not just about passing on knowledge; it's about loving people, walking with them, and helping them grow in their relationship with Christ. It's about breaking down barriers, tearing down walls of division, and showing people that in Christ, they are loved, accepted, and included. Paul's life also shows us that teaching the Gospel requires sacrifice. It's not always easy, and it often involves suffering, but it's worth it because the message we carry has the power to change lives for eternity. As a teacher of the Gentiles, Paul didn't shy away from the hard work of ministry. He didn't avoid the difficult conversations or the challenging situations. He was willing to confront false teachings, to correct errors, and to stand up for the truth of the Gospel, even when it was unpopular or dangerous. He knew that the souls of the Gentiles were at stake, and he was determined to do everything in his power to ensure that they heard and understood the message of Jesus Christ. Paul's role as a teacher of the Gentiles also teaches us about the importance of perseverance. Paul faced immense opposition, both from within the church and from the outside world, but he never gave up. He kept teaching, kept preaching, kept sharing the Gospel, even when it seemed like no one was listening. In 2 Timothy 4:7, as Paul reflects on his life, he writes, "I have fought a good fight, I have finished my course, I have kept the faith." Paul's perseverance in his mission to teach the Gentiles is an inspiration to us all, reminding us that no matter how difficult the journey, we must remain faithful to the calling God has given us. As a teacher of the Gentiles, Paul's legacy continues to impact the world today. His letters, filled with wisdom, encouragement, and deep theological insight, continue to guide and instruct believers around the globe. The truths he taught about grace, faith, unity, and the power of the Holy Spirit are as relevant today as they were in the first century, and they continue to inspire and challenge us to live lives fully devoted to Christ. Paul's life as a teacher of the Gentiles was one of deep love, unwavering commitment, and faithful service to God and His people. He was a man transformed by the grace of God, and through that transformation, he became a vessel through which the Gospel was brought to the ends of the earth. His example calls us to be teachers of the Gospel in our own lives, to share the message of Jesus with those around us, and to live lives that reflect the love and grace of the Savior we serve. Paul's life as a teacher of the Gentiles is a powerful reminder that the Gospel is for everyone, and that we are all called to be part of God's mission to bring His message of hope and salvation to a lost and broken world.

Chapter 9 - Bondservant of Christ

In Galatians 1:10, the Apostle Paul writes, "For do I now persuade men, or God? or do I seek to please men? for if I yet pleased men, I should not be the servant of Christ." In this powerful verse, Paul refers to himself as a servant—or more accurately, a bondservant—of Christ. This term "bondservant" in the ancient world referred to someone who had willingly given themselves up to serve their master for life, bound not by force but by choice and devotion. When Paul calls himself a bondservant of Christ, it shows his deep, personal commitment and surrender to Jesus. It wasn't about gaining the approval of people or seeking recognition, but about total submission to the will of God. A bondservant didn't have his own agenda, desires, or plans; his life was entirely dedicated to serving his master's purpose. For Paul, being a bondservant of Christ meant that every aspect of his life was surrendered to the Lordship of Jesus. His identity, his mission, his purpose, and even his suffering were all tied to serving Christ. Imagine the emotional weight of such a calling—the deep sense of purpose, mixed with the trials and sacrifices, but also the unshakeable joy that comes from knowing that you are living completely for the glory of God.

Paul's journey to becoming a bondservant of Christ was not an easy or comfortable one. Before his conversion, he was known as Saul, a zealous Pharisee who fiercely persecuted Christians, thinking he was doing God's will by trying to stamp out what he saw as a dangerous heresy. But everything changed when Paul encountered the risen Jesus on the road to Damascus. In that moment, he was struck blind, but it was in his blindness that Paul truly saw for the first time. He realized that the very Jesus he was persecuting was the true Messiah, the Savior of the world. Paul's heart was transformed, and from that moment on, his life was no longer his own—it belonged completely to Christ. He went from being a persecutor of the church to being its most passionate defender and missionary, traveling across the Roman Empire to preach the Gospel, plant churches, and disciple believers. But through it all, Paul understood that his life was no longer about seeking his own glory or pleasing others—it was about serving Christ as His bondservant.

Being a bondservant of Christ wasn't just a title for Paul; it was the core of his identity. It meant total allegiance to Jesus, no matter the cost. In Galatians 1:10, Paul makes it clear that he wasn't living to please men or to gain the approval of others. He didn't change his message to fit the expectations of people. He wasn't swayed by popularity or the opinions of the world. His sole purpose was to do the will of God. To be a bondservant of Christ means to live with an audience of One, to be more concerned with God's approval than man's praise. This kind of devotion requires a heart that is fully surrendered, a life that is willing to sacrifice everything for the sake of Christ. Paul knew that being a bondservant of Christ would lead to hardship, suffering, and persecution, but he embraced it joyfully because he knew that serving Christ was worth it. The world around him might have mocked or rejected him, but Paul's eyes were fixed on Jesus, and he was determined to remain faithful to the One who had saved him.

Paul's life as a bondservant of Christ was marked by deep humility and unwavering commitment. As a bondservant, Paul didn't see himself as someone to be admired or exalted; he saw himself as a servant of the One who deserved all the glory. In Philippians 2:7-8, Paul writes of Jesus, "But made himself of no reputation, and took upon him the form of a servant, and was made in the likeness of men: And being found in fashion as a man, he humbled himself, and became obedient unto death, even the death of the cross." Paul's understanding of what it meant to be a servant of Christ was shaped by the example of Jesus Himself. Jesus, the Son of God, had humbled Himself to the point of death on the cross, taking on the role of a servant to save humanity. Paul followed in His footsteps, recognizing that his calling as a bondservant of Christ was to serve others, to lay down his life for the sake of the Gospel, and to live in humility, knowing that any honor or recognition belonged to Christ alone.

As a bondservant of Christ, Paul's life was one of total devotion and sacrifice. He endured beatings, imprisonment, shipwrecks, hunger, and danger for the sake of the Gospel. In 2 Corinthians 11:24-28, Paul recounts the sufferings he endured, saying, "Of the Jews five times received I forty stripes save one. Thrice was I beaten with rods, once was I stoned, thrice I suffered shipwreck, a night and a day I have been in the deep; In journeyings often, in perils of waters, in perils of robbers, in perils by mine own countrymen, in perils by the heathen, in perils in the city, in perils in the wilderness, in perils in the sea, in perils among false brethren; In weariness and painfulness, in watchings often, in hunger and thirst, in fastings often, in cold and nakedness." Yet through all of this, Paul never wavered. He understood that his life was not his own—it belonged to Christ. He wasn't driven by comfort, success, or personal gain; he was driven by the love of Christ and the desire to serve Him with everything he had. Paul's life as a bondservant of Christ challenges us to examine our own hearts and our own commitment to the Lord. Are we willing to lay down our lives, our plans, our desires, to follow Christ fully? Are we willing to serve Him, not out of obligation, but out of love and gratitude for what He has done for us?

Paul's bondservanthood was rooted in a deep understanding of grace. He knew that he had been saved not because of anything he had done, but because of the mercy and grace of God. In 1 Timothy 1:15, Paul writes, "This is a faithful saying, and worthy of all acceptation, that Christ Jesus came into the world to save sinners; of whom I am chief." Paul never forgot where he had come from. He knew that he had once been an enemy of Christ, but through God's grace, he had been forgiven, redeemed, and called to serve as a bondservant of Christ. This understanding of grace fueled Paul's passion for the Gospel and his commitment to serving Christ. He was deeply aware of the incredible gift of salvation he had received, and that awareness drove him to give his life completely to the One who had saved him.

Being a bondservant of Christ also meant that Paul's priorities were radically different from those of the world. He wasn't interested in wealth, power, or prestige. His treasure was not in earthly possessions but in the eternal rewards of serving Christ. In Philippians 3:7-8, Paul writes, "But what things were gain to me, those I counted loss for Christ. Yea doubtless, and I count all things but loss for the excellency of the knowledge of Christ Jesus my Lord: for whom I have suffered the loss of all things, and do count them but dung, that I may win Christ." Paul considered everything else in his life as nothing compared to the surpassing worth of knowing and serving Jesus. He was willing to give up everything—his status, his comfort, even his very life—because he knew that what he gained in Christ was far greater than anything this world could offer.

Paul's life as a bondservant of Christ also shows us the power of freedom through surrender. In the world's eyes, being a servant might seem like a loss of freedom, but for Paul, it was the greatest freedom he could ever experience. By surrendering his life to Christ, Paul was no longer a slave to sin, fear, or the opinions of others. He was free to live fully for the glory of God, knowing that his life was in the hands of a loving and faithful Master. In Romans 6:22, Paul writes, "But now being made free from sin, and become servants to God, ye have your fruit unto holiness, and the end everlasting life." Paul understood that true freedom comes not from living for ourselves, but from living for Christ. As a bondservant of Christ, Paul experienced the joy and fulfillment of knowing that his life had purpose, meaning, and eternal significance.

As we reflect on Paul's life as a bondservant of Christ, we are reminded of the call on each of our lives to follow Jesus with that same devotion and surrender. Being a bondservant of Christ means giving up our own will and desires to follow His will for our lives. It means living with an eternal perspective, knowing that our ultimate reward is not in this life but in the life to come. It means finding our identity, purpose, and joy in serving Christ, knowing that He is a faithful Master who loves us and has a perfect plan for our lives. Paul's life is a powerful example of what it means to be fully surrendered to Christ, to live not for the approval of men, but for the glory of God. His story challenges us to ask ourselves: Are we living as bondservants of Christ? Are we willing to give up everything to follow Him? Paul's life shows us that the cost of following Christ may be great, but the reward is far greater. When we live as bondservants of Christ, we find true freedom, true joy, and true purpose, knowing that our lives are in the hands of the One who gave His life for us.

In the end, Paul's life as a bondservant of Christ is a beautiful and inspiring picture of what it means to live a life fully devoted to Jesus. It is a life marked by sacrifice, humility, and unwavering commitment to the Gospel. It is a life that challenges us to lay down our own desires and to take up the call to serve Christ with everything we have. Paul's story reminds us that being a bondservant of Christ is not a burden, but a privilege—a privilege to serve the King of kings and to be a part of His eternal plan. It is a life that is rich with meaning, purpose, and joy, and it is a life that ultimately brings glory to God. As we look at Paul's life, we are reminded of the words of Jesus in Matthew 16:24-25: "If any man will come after me, let him deny himself, and take up his cross, and follow me. For whosoever will save his life shall lose it: and whosoever will lose his life for my sake shall find it." Paul's life as a bondservant of Christ is a testimony to the truth of those words, and it calls us to follow in his footsteps, living our lives fully surrendered to the One who gave His life for us.

Chapter 10 - Witness to the Resurrection

In Acts 26:16, the risen Jesus speaks directly to Paul during his dramatic conversion, saying, "But rise, and stand upon thy feet: for I have appeared unto thee for this purpose, to make thee a minister and a witness both of these things which thou hast seen, and of those things in the which I will appear unto thee." In this powerful moment, Paul is chosen to be a "witness to the resurrection," a witness of the risen Christ who conquered death and brought life and hope to the world. Imagine the awe and fear Paul must have felt as he, who had once been a fierce persecutor of Christians, now stood in the glorious presence of the very Jesus he had opposed. This experience was not just a vision or an encounter; it was a life-altering commission, calling Paul to testify to the truth that Jesus Christ was alive, risen from the dead, and reigning as the Savior and Lord. To be a witness to the resurrection was not simply to speak of an event from history, but to bear witness to the very heart of the Christian faith—the reality that death had been defeated, that sin's power was broken, and that Jesus Christ was victorious over the grave. For Paul, this calling was not just about recounting the facts of the resurrection; it was about proclaiming the transformative power of Jesus' victory over death and the new life that comes through Him.

From the moment Paul encountered the risen Jesus on the road to Damascus, his life was forever changed. He went from being Saul, a man zealous for the law and determined to destroy the early Christian movement, to Paul, an apostle of grace, love, and truth. His mission was clear: he was to be a witness to the resurrection, telling the world that Jesus was not dead, but alive—alive and bringing salvation to all who would believe in Him. This was a message that turned the world upside down. The resurrection was not just a story to be told; it was the foundation of everything Paul preached. Without the resurrection, there was no Gospel, no good news, no hope. But because

Jesus had risen from the dead, everything was different. Paul's message was not about rules or rituals, but about a living, breathing relationship with the risen Christ, who had conquered sin and death and offered eternal life to all who would trust in Him. To be a witness to the resurrection meant that Paul's entire life was now centered on the risen Christ. It wasn't just something he believed in; it was something that transformed every fiber of his being. The resurrection of Jesus gave Paul a new identity, a new purpose, and a new mission. He was no longer Saul the persecutor, but Paul the apostle, chosen by God to carry the message of the resurrection to the Gentiles, to kings, and to the children of Israel.

Paul's role as a witness to the resurrection was both a great privilege and a great responsibility. He was not just called to preach about the resurrection; he was called to live in its power. The resurrection was not just a theological concept for Paul—it was the very power that sustained him through every trial, every persecution, and every hardship he faced. In 2 Corinthians 4:10-11, Paul writes, "Always bearing about in the body the dying of the Lord Jesus, that the life also of Jesus might be made manifest in our body. For we which live are alway delivered unto death for Jesus' sake, that the life also of Jesus might be made manifest in our mortal flesh." Paul understood that being a witness to the resurrection meant living a life that reflected the power of Jesus' victory over death. It meant that even in the midst of suffering, pain, and persecution, the life of Christ was at work in him, giving him strength, hope, and joy. Paul's life was a living testimony to the truth of the resurrection. Every time he endured beatings, imprisonments, shipwrecks, and even death threats, he was bearing witness to the power of the risen Christ within him. He knew that no matter what happened to his body, his soul was secure in Christ, because Jesus had defeated death once and for all. This gave Paul the courage to stand before kings, rulers, and hostile crowds, proclaiming with boldness that Jesus was alive and offering salvation to all.

As a witness to the resurrection, Paul's life was filled with a sense of urgency and purpose. He knew that the message of the resurrection was the most important truth the world could ever hear, and he was willing to give everything to make sure that people knew that Jesus was alive. In 1 Corinthians 15:14-15, Paul writes, "And if Christ be not risen, then is our preaching vain, and your faith is also vain. Yea, and we are found false witnesses of God;

because we have testified of God that he raised up Christ." Paul understood that everything hinged on the resurrection. Without it, there was no Gospel. But because Jesus had risen, Paul's preaching had power, and his witness was true. He wasn't just telling people about a dead Savior; he was introducing them to a living Lord who had the power to change their lives, just as He had changed Paul's. Paul's witness to the resurrection wasn't just about telling others what had happened; it was about inviting them into the reality of the resurrection, inviting them to experience the new life, the forgiveness, and the hope that comes through faith in the risen Jesus.

Paul's life as a witness to the resurrection was also a life marked by deep love and compassion. He knew that the resurrection wasn't just good news for a select few; it was good news for everyone. Jesus' victory over death meant that all people—Jew and Gentile, rich and poor, slave and free—could come to God and receive eternal life. This is why Paul's mission was to take the message of the resurrection to the ends of the earth, to preach it to every nation, every tribe, and every people. Paul's heart burned with a desire to see people set free from the bondage of sin and death, and he knew that the resurrection was the key to that freedom. In Romans 10:9, Paul writes, "That if thou shalt confess with thy mouth the Lord Jesus, and shalt believe in thine heart that God hath raised him from the dead, thou shalt be saved." The resurrection was the very heart of Paul's message of salvation. It wasn't just a historical event; it was the reality that brought salvation to all who would believe.

Paul's witness to the resurrection was not without opposition. He faced fierce resistance from both Jews and Gentiles who found the message of the resurrection either offensive or foolish. The idea that a man could rise from the dead was a stumbling block to many, and Paul often found himself ridiculed, rejected, and even persecuted for his testimony. But Paul never wavered in his witness. He knew that the resurrection was the truth, and he was willing to suffer and even die for that truth. In Acts 20:24, Paul says, "But none of these things move me, neither count I my life dear unto myself, so that I might finish my course with joy, and the ministry, which I have received of the Lord Jesus, to testify the gospel of the grace of God." Paul's witness to the resurrection was driven by an unwavering commitment to the truth of the Gospel and a deep love for the people he was called to reach. He was willing to endure any hardship, any suffering, and even death itself, because he knew that the message of the resurrection was worth it.

Being a witness to the resurrection also gave Paul an unshakable hope. He knew that because Jesus had risen from the dead, death no longer had the final say. In 1 Corinthians 15:54-55, Paul triumphantly declares, "Death is swallowed up in victory. O death, where is thy sting? O grave, where is thy victory?" Paul's witness to the resurrection was not just about what happened to Jesus; it was about the promise of resurrection for all who believe in Him. Paul knew that because Jesus had conquered death, all who trusted in Him would one day be raised to eternal life. This hope gave Paul the strength to endure the hardships of this life, knowing that his future was secure in Christ. No matter what trials or sufferings he faced, Paul knew that the resurrection had the final word, and that gave him a deep and abiding joy.

Paul's role as a witness to the resurrection wasn't just about preaching or teaching; it was about living in the power of the resurrection every day. The resurrection wasn't just an event in the past; it was the reality that shaped every moment of Paul's life. It was the reason he could face danger with courage, endure suffering with patience, and continue preaching the Gospel with passion, even when it seemed like no one was listening. The power of the resurrection was at work in Paul, giving him strength when he was weak, hope when he was discouraged, and joy in the midst of trials. In Philippians 3:10-11, Paul writes, "That I may know him, and the power of his resurrection, and the fellowship of his sufferings, being made conformable unto his death; If by any means I might attain unto the resurrection of the dead." For Paul, being a witness to the resurrection wasn't just about telling others what had happened; it was about living in the reality of the resurrection, allowing the power of the risen Christ to shape every aspect of his life.

As a witness to the resurrection, Paul's life continues to inspire and challenge us today. His unwavering commitment to the truth of the resurrection, his boldness in proclaiming the Gospel, and his deep love for people are examples for us to follow. Paul's witness reminds us that the resurrection is not just a story from the past; it is the foundation of our faith, the source of our hope, and the power that enables us to live for Christ every day. Just as Paul was called to be a witness to the resurrection, we too are called to bear witness to the risen Christ in our own lives. We are called to proclaim the good news that Jesus is alive, that He has defeated death, and that through Him, we can have eternal life. Paul's life as a witness to the resurrection is a powerful testimony to the truth of the Gospel and a reminder that the resurrection changes everything. It is the reason we can face the challenges of this life with hope, knowing that our future is secure in Christ, and that one day, we too will be raised to new life with Him.

Chapter 11 - Persecutor Turned Apostle

In 1 Corinthians 15:9-10, Paul writes, "For I am the least of the apostles, that I am not meet to be called an apostle, because I persecuted the church of God. But by the grace of God I am what I am: and his grace which was bestowed upon me was not in vain; but I laboured more abundantly than they all: yet not I, but the grace of God which was with me." These verses tell the powerful story of transformation, a story of a man who went from being a fierce persecutor of the church to one of its most passionate apostles. Paul's life stands as a beacon of hope, a vivid reminder that no one is too far gone for God's grace to reach. In fact, it was Paul's very past—his violent opposition to the early Christian movement—that made his conversion so astounding. Imagine the emotional and spiritual weight that Paul must have carried, knowing that he had once been responsible for the suffering and imprisonment of countless Christians, yet now he was called to be one of the most significant leaders of the faith he had tried to destroy. Paul's story is one of radical grace, a grace so profound that it not only forgave him but also transformed him into a vessel of God's power and love. When Paul calls himself "the least of the apostles," he isn't being overly humble—he is reflecting on the truth of where he had come from. He knew that by human standards, he didn't deserve to be called an apostle. He had spent years zealously hunting down Christians, driven by what he thought was righteous zeal to preserve the traditions of Judaism. He was present at the stoning of Stephen, the first Christian martyr, giving his approval as a man's life was brutally taken for his faith in Jesus. But what makes Paul's story so compelling is not where he started, but how his life was utterly transformed by an encounter with the risen Christ on the road to Damascus. That moment was a turning point not only in Paul's life but in the history of the church.

Before his conversion, Paul, then known as Saul, was a man who lived by the law. He was a Pharisee, strict in his observance of the Jewish law, and fiercely protective of the traditions of his ancestors. He was a man who believed he was right, who believed that the followers of Jesus were dangerous heretics who needed to be stopped. His zeal for God, though sincere, was tragically misplaced, and it led him to become one of the greatest persecutors of the early church. But then, on the road to Damascus, everything changed. In a blinding flash of light, Paul was confronted by the risen Jesus. In that moment, he was not just blinded physically, but spiritually awakened. He heard the voice of Jesus saying, "Saul, Saul, why persecutest thou me?" (Acts 9:4). Those words cut deep, and Paul realized that in persecuting the followers of Jesus, he was actually fighting against God Himself. The very Lord he had rejected and opposed was now calling him into His service. This moment of confrontation became a moment of grace, a moment when Paul's entire world was turned upside down. The man who had once been the fiercest enemy of the church was now being called to be its most passionate advocate.

Paul's transformation from persecutor to apostle is one of the most powerful stories of redemption in all of Scripture. It shows us that no one is beyond the reach of God's grace, that no sin is too great to be forgiven, and that no past is too dark for God to use for His glory. Paul didn't just become a believer in Jesus—he became a tireless missionary, traveling across the Roman Empire, preaching the Gospel, planting churches, and writing letters that would form a significant portion of the New Testament. The very man who had once sought to destroy the church now became its most ardent defender and teacher. In 1 Corinthians 15:10, Paul acknowledges the source of this transformation: "But by the grace of God I am what I am." Paul knew that it wasn't his own doing that had brought about this change. It wasn't because he had suddenly become a better person or because he had earned his place among the apostles. It was purely and simply by the grace of God. Paul's story is a testament to the power of grace, to the truth that it is God who chooses and calls, not based on our worthiness, but based on His love and purpose.

Paul's conversion didn't erase the pain of his past, but it redeemed it. He carried the memories of his former life with him, but those memories were no longer a source of shame—they became a backdrop against which the grace of God shone all the brighter. Paul's life demonstrates that God can take the most broken, sinful, and hardened heart and transform it into something beautiful for His kingdom. Paul's past as a persecutor didn't disqualify him from being an apostle; instead, it became a platform for him to testify to the greatness of God's mercy. When Paul preached about grace, he spoke from personal experience. He knew what it meant to be forgiven much, and that knowledge fueled his passion for the Gospel. He labored tirelessly, not to earn God's favor, but because he had already received it. In every city he visited, every church he planted, and every letter he wrote, Paul was driven by the overwhelming grace that had been poured out on him. He wanted everyone to know that the same grace that had transformed his life was available to all.

Being an apostle wasn't easy for Paul. He faced constant opposition, persecution, and suffering. He was beaten, imprisoned, stoned, shipwrecked, and eventually martyred for his faith. But through it all, Paul never lost sight of the grace that had called him. He knew that everything he endured was worth it because of the surpassing value of knowing Christ and making Him known. Paul's story as a persecutor turned apostle is a story of hope for all of us. It shows us that God's grace is greater than our sin, that His power is made perfect in our weakness, and that He can use even the darkest parts of our past for His glory. Paul's life is a reminder that no matter where we've been or what we've done, God can still use us in incredible ways.

Paul's transformation also teaches us about the humility that comes from understanding grace. In 1 Corinthians 15:9, Paul refers to himself as "the least of the apostles." This wasn't false humility—Paul truly understood the depth of his own unworthiness. He knew that by human standards, he had no right to be called an apostle. But it was precisely this awareness of his own unworthiness that made Paul such a powerful instrument of God's grace. He didn't boast in his own abilities or accomplishments; he boasted in the grace of God that had worked through him. Paul's humility wasn't a weakness—it was a strength. It allowed him to depend fully on God and to give all the glory to Him. Paul's life shows us that when we understand the depth of our own need for grace, we are freed from the need to prove ourselves or to earn our place. We can rest in the knowledge that God's grace is enough, and that He has chosen us, not because of who we are, but because of who He is.

Paul's story also challenges us to consider how we view others. It's easy to write people off as hopeless, to assume that they are too far gone for God to reach. But Paul's life reminds us that no one is beyond the reach of God's grace. If God can transform a man like Paul—a man who was actively persecuting the church—He can transform anyone. Paul's story encourages us to pray for those who seem far from God, to believe that His grace can break through even the hardest hearts, and to trust that He is always at work, even in the most unlikely places. It also challenges us to extend grace to others, knowing that we have been recipients of God's incredible mercy.

Paul's transformation from persecutor to apostle is a story that continues to inspire and encourage believers today. It is a story of redemption, hope, and the unstoppable power of God's grace. It shows us that God delights in using the weak, the broken, and the flawed to accomplish His purposes. Paul's life reminds us that our past does not define us—God's grace does. It reminds us that we are not disqualified by our failures, but that God can use even our worst mistakes to bring about His glory. Paul's story is a testament to the truth that God's grace is always greater than our sin, that His love is always stronger than our failures, and that His plans for us are always bigger than we can imagine.

As we reflect on Paul's journey from persecutor to apostle, we are reminded of the power of God's transforming grace. Paul's life is a living testimony to the truth that "where sin abounded, grace did much more abound" (Romans 5:20). His story is one of hope for all who feel unworthy, for all who feel that their past disqualifies them from being used by God. Paul's life shows us that God specializes in redeeming the broken, in using the unlikely, and in transforming the unworthy. He takes our failures, our sins, and our mistakes, and He uses them to showcase His incredible grace and mercy. Paul's life is a powerful reminder that it's not about who we were, but about who God is making us to be. In Christ, we are new creations, and God can use our lives—no matter where we've been—to bring glory to His name and to advance His kingdom.

In the end, Paul's story as a persecutor turned apostle is a story of grace—grace that forgives, grace that transforms, and grace that empowers. It is a story that reminds us that God's grace is never in vain. Just as God's grace was not wasted on Paul, it is not wasted on us. He has a purpose and a plan for each of our lives, and when we surrender to His grace, He can use us in ways we never thought possible. Paul's life is a testament to the truth that God's grace is always greater than our past, and that through His grace, we can be transformed into vessels of His love and truth, just as Paul was transformed into a witness of the Gospel and an apostle of Jesus Christ.

Chapter 12 - Founder of Churches

In 1 Corinthians 3:10, Paul writes, "According to the grace of God which is given unto me, as a wise masterbuilder, I have laid the foundation, and another buildeth thereon. But let every man take heed how he buildeth thereupon." This verse powerfully expresses Paul's role as a founder of churches, a responsibility he did not take lightly, and one that was only made possible through the grace of God. Paul refers to himself as a "wise masterbuilder," acknowledging that it was by God's wisdom and strength that he was able to lay the foundation of churches throughout the Roman Empire. Paul's entire life and ministry were devoted to spreading the Gospel, planting churches in cities and regions that had never heard the name of Jesus. He was a trailblazer, a pioneer of the faith, carrying the good news of Jesus Christ to Gentiles and Jews alike, establishing communities of believers that would become the heart of Christianity for generations to come. To be a founder of churches wasn't simply about establishing physical places where people gathered—it was about laying the spiritual groundwork for the Kingdom of God on earth, creating a foundation on which the faith of countless people would be built. Paul knew that the foundation he was laying was not built on his own abilities or charisma, but on Christ, the chief cornerstone (Ephesians 2:20). The foundation of every church Paul established was the Gospel of Jesus Christ, the message of salvation by grace through faith, and the promise of new life in Christ. Paul's life as a founder of churches was a life of relentless passion, deep sacrifice, and unwavering commitment to the mission God had given him.

Paul's calling to be a founder of churches was a divine commission that shaped every aspect of his life. From the moment he encountered the risen Christ on the road to Damascus, Paul's heart burned with the desire to share the Gospel with as many people as possible, to see communities of believers rise up in cities and regions that had been steeped in paganism, idolatry, and spiritual darkness. His love for the church, for the body of Christ, was evident in everything he did. He didn't just plant churches and move on; he remained deeply connected to the churches he founded, nurturing them with his prayers, letters, and personal visits. His epistles, which make up a large portion of the New Testament, are filled with guidance, encouragement, correction, and instruction for the churches he had planted. Paul's heart was not only to bring people to Christ but to see them grow in their faith, to build up strong, healthy churches that would endure the test of time and trials. He often referred to the believers in the churches he founded as his spiritual children, showing the depth of his love and care for them. In 1 Thessalonians 2:7-8, Paul writes, "But we were gentle among you, even as a nurse cherisheth her children: So being affectionately desirous of you, we were willing to have imparted unto you, not the gospel of God only, but also our own souls, because ye were dear unto us." Paul didn't just preach to people; he invested his whole life into them, pouring out his heart and soul so that they could know Christ and grow in their relationship with Him.

As a founder of churches, Paul faced immense challenges. The world he was ministering to was filled with opposition—both spiritual and physical. He entered cities where paganism, immorality, and idolatry were deeply entrenched. In some places, Paul was welcomed with open hearts, but in many others, he was met with hostility, ridicule, and persecution. Yet, he pressed on, undeterred by the opposition he faced. He endured beatings, imprisonment, stonings, and rejection, all for the sake of the Gospel and the churches he was called to establish. In 2 Corinthians 11:24-28, Paul recounts the hardships he faced, saying, "Of the Jews five times received I forty stripes save one. Thrice was I beaten with rods, once was I stoned, thrice I suffered shipwreck, a night and a day I have been in the deep; In journeyings often, in perils of waters, in perils of robbers, in perils by mine own countrymen, in perils by the heathen, in perils in the city, in perils in the wilderness, in perils in the sea, in perils among false brethren; In weariness and painfulness, in watchings often, in hunger and thirst, in fastings often, in cold and nakedness. Beside those things that are without, that which cometh upon me daily, the care of all the churches." Paul's life was one of total dedication to Christ and His church. He was willing to endure any hardship, any suffering, for the sake of building up the body of Christ.

The foundation that Paul laid as a founder of churches was rooted in the unshakable truth of the Gospel. He knew that the only foundation that could sustain the church was Jesus Christ. In 1 Corinthians 3:11, Paul writes, "For other foundation can no man lay than that is laid, which is Jesus Christ." Paul's role as a founder wasn't about creating something of his own; it was about pointing people to Christ, making sure that their faith was built on Him alone. Paul was deeply concerned with the spiritual health of the churches he founded. He knew that false teachings, divisions, and sin could easily creep in and threaten to undermine the foundation he had laid. That's why he constantly reminded the believers to stay rooted in the truth of the Gospel, to hold fast to their faith in Christ, and to live lives worthy of their calling. His letters are filled with warnings against false teachers, encouragement to remain steadfast in the faith, and instructions on how to live as followers of Jesus. Paul understood that the church wasn't just a collection of individuals; it was the body of Christ, and each believer was a vital part of that body. He taught the churches about unity, about the importance of love and humility, and about using their spiritual gifts to build up one another.

Paul's role as a founder of churches was not just about starting something new—it was about building something that would last. He wasn't interested in short-term success or in numbers; he was focused on making disciples, on creating communities of believers who would grow in their faith and continue the work of the Gospel long after he was gone. Paul's vision for the church was long-term. He knew that the churches he founded would face trials, persecutions, and temptations, but he also knew that if they were built on the foundation of Christ, they would stand strong. In Ephesians 4:12-13, Paul speaks of his desire for the church, saying that God gave apostles, prophets, evangelists, pastors, and teachers "for the perfecting of the saints, for the work of the ministry, for the edifying of the body of Christ: Till we all come in the unity of the faith, and of the knowledge of the Son of God, unto a perfect man, unto the measure of the stature of the fulness of Christ." Paul wanted the churches he founded to grow in maturity, to become fully formed in their faith, and to reflect the character of Christ in everything they did.

As a founder of churches, Paul's legacy extends far beyond the first century. The churches he planted in cities like Corinth, Ephesus, Philippi, Thessalonica, and others became the heart of the early Christian movement. His letters to these churches have shaped Christian theology, practice, and community for nearly two thousand years. The foundation that Paul laid through his ministry continues to bear fruit today, as countless believers around the world have come to know Christ and have grown in their faith through the churches he founded and the letters he wrote. Paul's life as a founder of churches reminds us that the work of the Gospel is never in vain. Every seed planted, every church founded, every life touched by the message of Christ has the potential to bear fruit for generations to come.

Paul's role as a founder of churches was not about personal glory or recognition. He didn't seek fame or accolades for himself. In fact, he often faced criticism and rejection, even from within the churches he founded. Yet, he remained focused on his mission, knowing that it was not about him, but about Christ. In Galatians 6:14, Paul writes, "But God forbid that I should glory, save in the cross of our Lord Jesus Christ, by whom the world is crucified unto me, and I unto the world." Paul's life was a testament to the truth that the foundation of the church is not built on human wisdom, strength, or ambition, but on the power of the cross. His only boast was in Christ, and his only goal was to see the name of Jesus lifted high and the church built up in faith and love.

As a founder of churches, Paul also knew the importance of raising up leaders. He understood that for the churches to thrive and continue to grow, they needed strong, faithful leaders who would shepherd the flock and teach the truth of the Gospel. Paul invested deeply in individuals like Timothy, Titus, and others, mentoring them, encouraging them, and entrusting them with the leadership of the churches. He saw the importance of equipping others to carry on the work of the ministry, and he was committed to building up the next generation of leaders who would continue the mission of the church. In 2 Timothy 2:2, Paul instructs Timothy, "And the things that thou hast heard of me among many witnesses, the same commit thou to faithful men, who shall be able to teach others also." Paul's vision for the church was not just about his own ministry; it was about ensuring that the Gospel would continue to be preached, that churches would continue to be founded, and that the faith would be passed on from generation to generation.

Paul's life as a founder of churches is a powerful example of what it means to be a servant of Christ, dedicated to the mission of the Gospel. His passion for the church, his willingness to sacrifice everything for the sake of the Gospel, and his unwavering commitment to building strong, healthy communities of believers inspire us to live with the same dedication and purpose. Paul's story challenges us to consider how we are contributing to the building up of the church. Are we investing in the lives of others, sharing the Gospel, and helping to lay a strong foundation for future generations? Paul's life reminds us that the church is not just a building or an institution—it is the body of Christ, and each of us has a role to play in its growth and flourishing.

In conclusion, Paul's role as a founder of churches was one of the most significant aspects of his ministry. Through the grace of God, Paul laid the foundation for churches that would change the world, bringing the message of Christ to countless people and establishing communities of faith that would endure for generations. His life as a "wise masterbuilder" teaches us about the importance of laying a strong foundation, one that is built on Christ and His Gospel. It reminds us that the work of the church is not easy, but it is worth every sacrifice. Paul's life of dedication, passion, and love for the church continues to inspire and challenge us today, calling us to be faithful in our own roles as builders of God's Kingdom, knowing that the foundation we lay in Christ will stand the test of time and bear fruit for eternity.

Chapter 13 - Steward of God's Mysteries

In 1 Corinthians 4:1, the Apostle Paul writes, "Let a man so account of us, as of the ministers of Christ, and stewards of the mysteries of God." These words give us a profound insight into Paul's self-understanding of his calling and role, not just as a preacher or apostle, but as a steward of God's mysteries. To be a steward in the biblical sense means to be entrusted with something precious that belongs to another, to guard and manage it faithfully. A steward doesn't own the treasure; they are responsible for caring for it, using it wisely, and sharing it at the right time. Paul saw himself as a steward of the greatest treasure of all—God's mysteries. These mysteries are not secret in the sense that they are hidden away, but rather, they are truths that were once unknown and have now been revealed by God through the Gospel of Jesus Christ. The greatest of these mysteries is the revelation of God's plan for salvation, that through the death and resurrection of Jesus, both Jew and Gentile can be reconciled to God and become one in Christ. For centuries, the world was in darkness about God's ultimate plan of redemption, but now, through Christ, the mystery has been unveiled, and Paul, as a steward, was tasked with the responsibility of sharing this revelation with the world. The weight of this responsibility was immense, but Paul embraced it fully, knowing that he had been entrusted with the message of life itself, the truth that could set souls free, reconcile sinners to God, and bring people from darkness into the light of Christ.

Imagine the overwhelming sense of awe that Paul must have felt, knowing that God had chosen him, a man who had once persecuted the church, to be a steward of these divine mysteries. Paul's past as a zealous Pharisee who sought to destroy the followers of Christ made his calling even more remarkable. Here was a man who had been blind—both physically and spiritually—until the day he encountered the risen Jesus on the road to Damascus. That encounter changed everything for Paul. His eyes were opened, not only to the reality of who Jesus was, but also to the depths of God's grace and the grandeur of His redemptive plan for humanity. Paul's life was turned upside down, and he realized that the very Gospel he had tried to destroy was, in fact, the fulfillment of God's promises from ages past. It was this Gospel—the good news of Jesus Christ—that Paul was now entrusted to share, and not just to his fellow Jews, but to the Gentiles, the very people who had once been considered outside of God's covenant. This was part of the great mystery that had been revealed to Paul, that in Christ, there is neither Jew nor Gentile, slave nor free, male nor female, but all are one in Him (Galatians 3:28). This mystery of unity in Christ, this message of salvation for all, was the treasure that Paul was called to steward, and he devoted his entire life to doing so faithfully.

As a steward of God's mysteries, Paul didn't merely preach a message—he lived it. He carried the burden of this stewardship with deep conviction and a sense of urgency, knowing that the Gospel had the power to change lives, to break chains of sin, and to bring eternal hope. In Ephesians 3:8-9, Paul writes, "Unto me, who am less than the least of all saints, is this grace given, that I should preach among the Gentiles the unsearchable riches of Christ; And to make all men see what is the fellowship of the mystery, which from the beginning of the world hath been hid in God, who created all things by Jesus Christ." Paul was humbled by the grace that had been given to him, that he, of all people, was entrusted with the glorious task of making known the unsearchable riches of Christ, to reveal the mystery that had been hidden for ages but was now made known through the Gospel. He didn't take this responsibility lightly. He understood that being a steward of God's mysteries meant not only proclaiming the truth but doing so with integrity, faithfulness, and love.

Paul's role as a steward required him to be diligent, wise, and courageous. The Gospel he proclaimed was often met with opposition. In some places, people received it with joy, but in many others, Paul was rejected, beaten, imprisoned, and ridiculed. Yet, he never wavered. He knew that the truth he carried was far too important to be silenced by fear or opposition. In 2 Corinthians 4:7-9, Paul writes, "But we have this treasure in earthen vessels, that the excellency of the power may be of God, and not of us. We are troubled on every side, yet not distressed; we are perplexed, but not in despair;

Persecuted, but not forsaken; cast down, but not destroyed." Paul recognized that he was merely an earthen vessel, fragile and imperfect, yet entrusted with the greatest treasure of all—the message of salvation in Christ. He knew that the power to change lives didn't come from him, but from God, and it was God's power working through him that enabled him to fulfill his calling as a steward of these divine mysteries.

As a steward, Paul also understood the importance of sharing the Gospel with clarity and purity. He was deeply concerned that the message of Christ not be distorted or watered down. In Galatians 1:8-9, Paul warns the church about the dangers of false gospels, saying, "But though we, or an angel from heaven, preach any other gospel unto you than that which we have preached unto you, let him be accursed." Paul knew that the truth of the Gospel was precious, and it had to be guarded and proclaimed faithfully. He didn't want anyone to add to it, take away from it, or twist it for personal gain. As a faithful steward, Paul was committed to protecting the purity of the Gospel message, ensuring that the churches he founded and the people he taught would receive the truth as it had been revealed by Christ.

Paul's stewardship of God's mysteries also involved a deep sense of love and care for the people to whom he ministered. He wasn't just concerned with delivering a message; he was deeply invested in the spiritual growth and well-being of the believers under his care. In Colossians 1:28-29, Paul writes, "Whom we preach, warning every man, and teaching every man in all wisdom; that we may present every man perfect in Christ Jesus: Whereunto I also labour, striving according to his working, which worketh in me mightily." Paul's goal as a steward of God's mysteries was not only to make the truth known but to help believers grow in their faith, to become mature in Christ. He labored tirelessly, striving with all his strength, to see that those under his care would be built up in their faith, grounded in the truth of the Gospel, and able to stand firm in the face of trials and temptations.

Paul's role as a steward was not without its burdens. He carried the weight of concern for the churches he had planted, the believers he had led to Christ, and the integrity of the Gospel message. In 2 Corinthians 11:28, Paul speaks of the daily pressure he felt: "Beside those things that are without, that which cometh upon me daily, the care of all the churches." Paul's stewardship wasn't just about preaching and teaching—it was about shepherding, nurturing, and protecting the flock of God. He felt a deep responsibility for the spiritual health of the churches he had established, and he spent countless hours in prayer, writing letters, and visiting these churches to ensure that they were growing in their faith and remaining true to the Gospel.

Being a steward of God's mysteries also meant that Paul had to endure suffering for the sake of the Gospel. He knew that his calling would not be easy. He faced opposition from both Jews and Gentiles, from religious leaders and government authorities, from false teachers and even from some within the church. But Paul understood that this was part of his stewardship. In Colossians 1:24, Paul writes, "Who now rejoice in my sufferings for you, and fill up that which is behind of the afflictions of Christ in my flesh for his body's sake, which is the church." Paul saw his sufferings as part of his stewardship, as a way of participating in the sufferings of Christ for the sake of the church. He was willing to endure anything, even death, if it meant that the Gospel would be proclaimed and that believers would be strengthened in their faith.

Paul's life as a steward of God's mysteries was a life of deep faith, tireless labor, and unwavering commitment to the truth of the Gospel. He knew that what had been entrusted to him was of eternal value, and he was determined to be found faithful in his stewardship. In 1 Corinthians 4:2, Paul writes, "Moreover it is required in stewards, that a man be found faithful." Faithfulness was at the heart of Paul's life and ministry. He wasn't interested in gaining popularity or wealth. He wasn't driven by a desire for power or influence. His only concern was to be faithful to the calling he had received, to proclaim the Gospel of Jesus Christ with integrity, courage, and love, and to help others come to know and grow in their relationship with Christ.

Paul's life as a steward of God's mysteries continues to inspire and challenge believers today. His example reminds us of the incredible responsibility and privilege we have as followers of Christ to steward the truth of the Gospel in our own lives. Like Paul, we are called to be faithful stewards, to share the good news of Jesus with others, to guard the purity of the Gospel, and to help others grow in their faith. Paul's life shows us that stewardship is not just about what we do with our time, talents, and resources—it's about how we handle the truth of God's Word, how we live out the Gospel in our daily lives, and how we invest in the spiritual growth of others.

As we reflect on Paul's life as a steward of God's mysteries, we are reminded that the Gospel is a treasure of inestimable worth, and we have been entrusted with it. Our calling, like Paul's, is to be faithful stewards, to guard the truth of the Gospel, to share it with those who have not yet heard, and to live in such a way that the power of Christ's death and resurrection is evident in our lives. Paul's life is a powerful testimony to the transformative power of the Gospel, the grace of God that can take a persecutor of the church and turn him into one of its greatest apostles, and the faithfulness of a man who understood the preciousness of what had been entrusted to him. His story calls us to take seriously our own stewardship of the Gospel, to live with the same passion, conviction, and faithfulness that Paul did, knowing that we, too, have been entrusted with the mysteries of God, and that our stewardship will have eternal consequences.

Chapter 14 - Spiritual Father

In 1 Corinthians 4:15, Paul writes, "For though ye have ten thousand instructors in Christ, yet have ye not many fathers: for in Christ Jesus I have begotten you through the gospel." These words reveal the deep and emotional heart of Paul's ministry as a spiritual father to the believers in Corinth, and by extension, to many others. The role of a spiritual father is not merely that of a teacher or instructor, but one of profound love, care, and personal investment. A father doesn't just impart knowledge; he nurtures, protects, and guides his children with a sacrificial love. Paul wasn't satisfied with just preaching the Gospel and leaving behind new believers to figure out their faith on their own. No, he saw them as his spiritual children, as those he had begotten through the Gospel, meaning that he played an intimate role in their spiritual birth and growth. He wasn't just their teacher; he was their father in the faith. To Paul, this meant far more than just giving them the basics of the Christian life—it meant walking with them, caring for them, disciplining them when needed, and encouraging them to grow into mature followers of Christ. The bond between Paul and the churches he planted was one of deep affection, responsibility, and love. He carried the weight of their spiritual well-being on his shoulders, not out of obligation, but out of a heart filled with love and concern for their souls. This role of spiritual fatherhood was not something Paul took lightly, for he understood that his task was not only to guide them in the truth but also to model Christ to them in his own life.

Being a spiritual father, as Paul describes, involves more than just instructing; it involves being a living example of what it means to follow Christ. In 1 Corinthians 11:1, Paul says, "Be ye followers of me, even as I also am of Christ." This statement reflects the heart of Paul's fatherly role—he wasn't asking the Corinthians to follow him for his sake, but to follow him as he followed Christ. Paul lived his life transparently before the believers, showing them through his actions, his sacrifices, and his love what it looked like to live a life surrendered to Jesus. He didn't lead from a distance; he was intimately involved in their lives, investing his time, his energy, and his very self into their spiritual growth. Paul's relationship with the Corinthians was personal. He had spent time with them, teaching them the Gospel, praying with them, and watching them grow in their faith. But like any father, Paul also had to correct them when they went astray. The church in Corinth struggled with many issues—division, immorality, pride—and Paul, as their spiritual father, wasn't afraid to confront these issues head-on. He did so, not out of harshness or anger, but out of a deep love for them, knowing that just as an earthly father disciplines his children for their good, so too must he guide and correct them for the sake of their spiritual health.

Paul's heart as a spiritual father can be seen in the way he grieved over the sins and struggles of the churches he had planted. In 2 Corinthians 11:28-29, Paul writes, "Beside those things that are without, that which cometh upon me daily, the care of all the churches. Who is weak, and I am not weak? who is offended, and I burn not?" Paul felt deeply the burdens and weaknesses of his spiritual children. When they stumbled, it pained him. When they were tempted or led astray, it stirred him to action. He wasn't indifferent to their struggles; he carried them in his heart and brought them before God in prayer. Like a father who worries for his children's safety, Paul worried for the spiritual well-being of the believers under his care. His letters are filled with expressions of concern, encouragement, and admonition, all flowing from a heart that was deeply invested in their growth in Christ.

But being a spiritual father also brought Paul great joy. He delighted in seeing his spiritual children grow in their faith, mature in their walk with Christ, and bear fruit for the Kingdom of God. In 1 Thessalonians 2:19-20, Paul writes, "For what is our hope, or joy, or crown of rejoicing? Are not even ye in the presence of our Lord Jesus Christ at his coming? For ye are our glory and joy." For Paul, the greatest joy and reward of his ministry was not in personal accolades or recognition, but in seeing those he had fathered in the faith stand firm in Christ. He saw their spiritual growth as his crowning achievement, the proof that his labor in the Lord had not been in vain. Like a father who beams with pride at his children's accomplishments, Paul found his joy in seeing the believers he had led to Christ walk faithfully in their new life.

Paul's role as a spiritual father was also marked by sacrifice. Just as a father sacrifices for the sake of his children, so too did Paul sacrifice for the sake of the churches. He endured incredible hardship—beatings, imprisonments, hunger, sleepless nights—all so that the Gospel could reach those who had not yet heard and so that the believers he had nurtured could continue to grow. In 2 Corinthians 12:15, Paul writes, "And I will very gladly spend and be spent for you; though the more abundantly I love you, the less I be loved." Paul's love for the churches wasn't conditional. He didn't love them because they loved him back; he loved them because they were his spiritual children, and he was willing to spend himself completely for their sake. His love was selfless, reflecting the love of Christ, who gave His life for the church. Paul's heart as a spiritual father was full of the same kind of sacrificial love, willing to endure whatever was necessary for the sake of the believers' growth in Christ.

Being a spiritual father, for Paul, also meant raising up others to carry on the work of the Gospel. He knew that his time on earth was limited, and that the work of the church would continue long after he was gone. So, like any good father, Paul invested in the next generation, raising up spiritual sons like Timothy and Titus to lead the church after him. In 1 Timothy 1:2, Paul calls Timothy his "own son in the faith," and throughout his letters, we see Paul mentoring, encouraging, and equipping Timothy to take on the mantle of leadership. Paul wasn't just concerned with the present; he was always looking to the future, making sure that the churches he had founded would be in good hands after his departure. This aspect of spiritual fatherhood is vital, as it ensures that the work of the Kingdom continues from generation to generation. Paul's investment in the lives of Timothy, Titus, and others was an extension of his role as a spiritual father, passing on the faith and ensuring that the Gospel would continue to spread long after his life had ended.

Paul's example as a spiritual father challenges us to consider how we are investing in the spiritual lives of others. Are we willing to pour ourselves into the lives of those around us, not just instructing them in the faith, but walking with them, loving them, and helping them grow in their relationship with Christ? Paul's life shows us that being a spiritual father—or mother—is not about authority or control; it's about love, sacrifice, and commitment. It's about being willing to lay down our lives for the sake of others, just as Christ laid down His life for us. Paul's heart for the church was a reflection of Christ's heart, and his life challenges us to live with the same kind of love and devotion to those whom God has placed in our care.

Paul's role as a spiritual father also reminds us of the importance of discipleship. He didn't just preach the Gospel and move on; he invested deeply in the lives of those he had led to Christ. He understood that spiritual growth takes time, care, and attention, and he was committed to walking alongside the believers he had fathered in the faith, helping them grow in their understanding of the Gospel and their walk with Christ. In 1 Corinthians 3:2, Paul speaks of how he had to feed the Corinthians with "milk, and not with meat," because they were still babes in Christ. Paul recognized that spiritual maturity doesn't happen overnight. Like a father who patiently teaches his children, Paul was patient with the believers, nurturing them and guiding them step by step as they grew in their faith.

As a spiritual father, Paul's ultimate goal was to see Christ formed in the lives of the believers. In Galatians 4:19, Paul writes, "My little children, of whom I travail in birth again until Christ be formed in you." This is the heart of spiritual fatherhood—laboring, praying, and working until the character of Christ is fully formed in the lives of those we disciple. Paul's desire wasn't just that the believers would know about Christ, but that they would become like Christ, that their lives would reflect His love, His holiness, and His grace. This is the ultimate goal of spiritual fatherhood, to see those we have nurtured in the faith grow into mature, Christlike followers of Jesus, fully equipped to carry on the work of the Gospel.

Paul's life as a spiritual father is a powerful example of what it means to invest in the lives of others for the sake of the Kingdom of God. His love, sacrifice, and commitment to the believers under his care remind us of the importance of relationships in the Christian life. We are not called to walk this journey of faith alone; we are called to walk together, to invest in one another, and to help each other grow in Christ. Paul's example challenges us to be intentional about our relationships, to look for opportunities to disciple and mentor others, and to be willing to pour ourselves into the lives of those God has entrusted to us.

In conclusion, Paul's role as a spiritual father, as described in 1 Corinthians 4:15, reveals the depth of his love and commitment to the believers he had led to Christ. He saw them not just as followers, but as his spiritual children, and he devoted his life to their growth in Christ. His example of spiritual fatherhood challenges us to live with the same kind of love, sacrifice, and commitment, investing in the spiritual lives of others and helping them grow into mature followers of Jesus. Paul's life reminds us that the work of the Gospel is not just about preaching or teaching—it's about relationships, about walking with others, and about helping them grow in their faith. His role as a spiritual father continues to inspire and challenge us today, calling us to invest deeply in the lives of those around us, so that Christ may be formed in them, and the Kingdom of God may continue to grow for generations to come.

Chapter 15 - Laborer in the Gospel

In 1 Thessalonians 2:9, Paul writes, "For ye remember, brethren, our labour and travail: for labouring night and day, because we would not be chargeable unto any of you, we preached unto you the gospel of God." These words give us a vivid glimpse into Paul's identity as a laborer in the Gospel, a title that reveals the depth of his dedication, sacrifice, and unwavering commitment to the work of the Lord. The image of a laborer in the Gospel is one of tireless effort, of someone who is fully engaged in the mission of preaching Christ, of building up the church, and of serving others without seeking anything in return. For Paul, this wasn't just a job or a temporary mission—it was his life's calling. He worked tirelessly, not for personal gain, but out of love for the people he ministered to and out of obedience to the Lord who had called him. Paul didn't see his role in the Gospel as something he did for his own benefit, nor did he preach for fame, wealth, or recognition. Instead, he labored with his whole heart and being, often through sleepless nights, hunger, suffering, and persecution, all for the sake of bringing the message of Jesus to as many people as possible. Paul's description of his labor speaks to the very heart of the Christian life, reminding us that to serve Christ is not a path of ease and comfort, but one of continual sacrifice, a life poured out for the sake of others, much like Christ Himself, who came not to be served but to serve and give His life as a ransom for many.

Paul's reference to "labour and travail" shows the physical, emotional, and spiritual cost of his ministry. The word "travail" evokes the image of childbirth, of the intense effort and pain that brings forth life. This is how Paul saw his work in the Gospel—it was laborious, exhausting, and often painful, but it was all worth it because through his labor, people were being born again into the Kingdom of God. Every time Paul shared the Gospel, every time he traveled to a new city, every time he endured hardship for the sake of Christ, he knew that his efforts were not in vain. His work was producing eternal results—lives were being transformed, souls were being saved, and the church was being built up. This is the essence of what it means to be a laborer in the Gospel. It is to give everything you have, knowing that the fruit of your labor is not temporary or fleeting, but eternal and glorious. Paul wasn't driven by earthly rewards or the approval of men; he was driven by the love of Christ and the knowledge that his labor was making an eternal impact.

Paul's labor in the Gospel was marked by selflessness. He worked "night and day," often not only preaching the Gospel but also supporting himself through tentmaking, so that he wouldn't be a burden to the people he ministered to. In 1 Corinthians 9:18, Paul says, "What is my reward then? Verily that, when I preach the gospel, I may make the gospel of Christ without charge, that I abuse not my power in the gospel." Paul's heart was to give freely, to labor without seeking anything in return, to ensure that no one could accuse him of preaching for personal gain. His only desire was to see people come to know Jesus, and he was willing to work with his hands, to go without sleep, and to endure hardship so that the Gospel could go forth unhindered. This attitude of selflessness is at the heart of what it means to be a true laborer in the Gospel. It's not about what we can get, but about what we can give. It's about pouring ourselves out for the sake of others, following the example of Christ, who gave everything for us.

Paul's labor was not without cost. He endured countless trials and sufferings for the sake of the Gospel. In 2 Corinthians 11:23-28, Paul lists some of the hardships he faced: "In labours more abundant, in stripes above measure, in prisons more frequent, in deaths oft. Of the Jews five times received I forty stripes save one. Thrice was I beaten with rods, once was I stoned, thrice I suffered shipwreck, a night and a day I have been in the deep... Beside those things that are without, that which cometh upon me daily, the care of all the churches." Paul's life was a life of suffering, not because he sought it out, but because he knew that the Gospel was worth every sacrifice. He didn't labor in vain; he labored with a deep sense of purpose, knowing that every trial he endured, every beating, every sleepless night was for the sake of Christ and the people he loved. Paul's example teaches us that laboring in the Gospel is not a glamorous or easy calling, but it is one that brings with it eternal joy and satisfaction because we are serving the King of kings and bringing others into His Kingdom.

Paul's labor was also marked by perseverance. No matter what he faced, Paul kept going. He was relentless in his mission to preach the Gospel to all people, no matter the cost. In Philippians 3:13-14, Paul writes, "Brethren, I count not myself to have apprehended: but this one thing I do, forgetting those things which are behind, and reaching forth unto those things which are before, I press toward the mark for the prize of the high calling of God in Christ Jesus." Paul never gave up. Even when he was imprisoned, even when he was beaten and left for dead, he pressed on because he knew that the work he was doing had eternal significance. He knew that his labor was not in vain, that every soul saved, every church planted, every life transformed was worth all the pain and suffering he endured. Paul's perseverance is a powerful example for all believers, reminding us that laboring in the Gospel requires endurance. We will face hardships, we will encounter opposition, but we must keep pressing forward, trusting that God will use our labor for His glory and the advancement of His Kingdom.

Paul's labor in the Gospel was also deeply personal. He didn't see his work as a job or a duty; he saw it as a calling, a privilege, and a joy. In Colossians 1:29, Paul writes, "Whereunto I also labour, striving according to his working, which worketh in me mightily." Paul knew that the strength for his labor didn't come from himself; it came from the Lord. He labored in the power of the Holy Spirit, trusting that God would give him the strength to fulfill his mission. This is a key aspect of what it means to be a laborer in the Gospel. We are not called to labor in our own strength, but in the strength that God provides. Paul's life shows us that when we rely on God's power, we can endure anything, and our labor will bear fruit because it is God working through us.

Paul's labor was also motivated by love. He loved the people he ministered to, and he was willing to lay down his life for them. In 2 Corinthians 12:15, Paul writes, "And I will very gladly spend and be spent for you; though the more abundantly I love you, the less I be loved." Paul's love for the church was a reflection of Christ's love, a love that is selfless, sacrificial, and unconditional. Paul didn't labor for recognition or for what he could get out of it; he labored because he loved God and loved people. His heart was to see people come to know Jesus, to grow in their faith, and to become mature followers of Christ. This love fueled his tireless work, his late nights, his travels, and his endurance through suffering. Paul's life challenges us to labor in the Gospel with the same kind of love, to pour ourselves out for others, knowing that every sacrifice is worth it because of the love of Christ.

Paul's labor in the Gospel was also deeply rooted in his understanding of the eternal reward that awaited him. In 2 Timothy 4:7-8, as Paul neared the end of his life, he wrote, "I have fought a good fight, I have finished my course, I have kept the faith: Henceforth there is laid up for me a crown of righteousness, which the Lord, the righteous judge, shall give me at that day." Paul knew that his labor in the Gospel was not in vain. He knew that every trial, every hardship, every act of service was being noticed by God and that one day he would receive the crown of righteousness. This eternal perspective gave Paul the strength to endure whatever came his way. He wasn't working for earthly rewards; he was working for a heavenly prize, knowing that the reward of seeing Christ face to face was worth every ounce of effort.

Paul's example as a laborer in the Gospel challenges us to examine our own lives and our own commitment to the work of the Lord. Are we willing to labor for the sake of the Gospel, even when it costs us? Are we willing to pour ourselves out for others, to work tirelessly for the sake of bringing the message of Jesus to those who have not yet heard? Paul's life reminds us that laboring in the Gospel is not just for pastors or missionaries; it is the calling of every believer. We are all called to be laborers in the vineyard of the Lord, to share the good news of Jesus with those around us, to serve others in love, and to build up the body of Christ.

Paul's labor in the Gospel also reminds us of the importance of community. He didn't labor alone. Throughout his letters, we see Paul working alongside other believers—Timothy, Silas, Barnabas, and many others. Paul understood that the work

of the Gospel was not meant to be done in isolation, but in partnership with others. He valued the fellowship of the believers, the support of his fellow workers, and the prayers of the churches. As laborers in the Gospel, we are called to work together, to support one another, to pray for one another, and to encourage one another in the work of the Lord. Paul's life reminds us that we are part of a larger body, and that together, we can accomplish far more for the Kingdom of God than we ever could alone.

In conclusion, Paul's role as a laborer in the Gospel, as described in 1 Thessalonians 2:9, reveals the heart of what it means to be a servant of Christ.

His life was one of tireless work, selfless sacrifice, and unwavering commitment to the mission of preaching the Gospel and building up the church. Paul's example challenges us to labor with the same dedication, perseverance, and love, knowing that our work for the Lord is not in vain. His life reminds us that laboring in the Gospel is not about seeking recognition or reward, but about serving others, sharing the love of Christ, and trusting that God will use our efforts for His glory and the advancement of His Kingdom. Paul's life as a laborer in the Gospel continues to inspire and challenge us today, calling us to give our all for the sake of Christ and to labor with joy, knowing that we are working for a heavenly prize that far outweighs any earthly reward.

Chapter 16 - Proclaimer of God's Grace

In Acts 20:24, Paul declares, "But none of these things move me, neither count I my life dear unto myself, so that I might finish my course with joy, and the ministry, which I have received of the Lord Jesus, to testify the gospel of the grace of God." This verse reveals the heart of Paul's life and mission as a proclaimer of God's grace, a title that captures the essence of everything he lived for, sacrificed for, and ultimately gave his life for. The grace of God was the driving force behind Paul's ministry, and he was consumed with a burning passion to proclaim this grace to the world, to tell everyone, everywhere, about the boundless, immeasurable love of God that is freely given through Jesus Christ. Paul understood that grace is at the very heart of the Gospel—God's unmerited favor, His gift of salvation that is offered to sinners who could never earn it or deserve it. This was the message that transformed Paul's own life, taking him from being a zealous persecutor of the church to becoming its most ardent apostle and missionary. The grace of God that Paul experienced on the road to Damascus changed everything for him, and from that moment on, his entire life was dedicated to sharing this grace with as many people as possible. To proclaim the grace of God wasn't just a task for Paul; it was the very purpose of his existence. He didn't just preach about grace; he lived it, breathed it, and embodied it in everything he did, knowing that the grace of God was the only hope for a lost and broken world.

Paul's understanding of grace was deeply personal. He knew firsthand what it meant to be a recipient of God's grace, to be forgiven, redeemed, and transformed by the love of Christ. In 1 Timothy 1:13-14, Paul writes, "Who was before a blasphemer, and a persecutor, and injurious: but I obtained mercy, because I did it ignorantly in unbelief. And the grace of our Lord was exceeding abundant with faith and love which is in Christ Jesus." Paul never forgot where he had come from—he had been an enemy of Christ, a man who had sought to destroy the very church he would one day give his life for. But God's grace reached down and rescued him, not because of anything Paul had done, but because of God's mercy and love. Paul's transformation from persecutor to apostle is one of the most powerful testimonies of grace in all of Scripture. It is a reminder that no one is too far gone for God's grace to reach. Paul's life became a living example of the truth that "where sin abounded, grace did much more abound" (Romans 5:20). This personal experience of grace fueled Paul's passion to proclaim it to others. He knew that if God's grace could save him, it could save anyone. This is why Paul's message was one of grace from beginning to end. He wasn't interested in preaching a gospel of works or human effort; he wanted people to know that salvation is a gift, freely given by God through Jesus Christ, and it can only be received by faith.

As a proclaimer of God's grace, Paul's message was radically different from the religious teachings of his day. The Jews were steeped in the law, believing that righteousness could be attained through strict adherence to the commandments. But Paul knew from his own experience that no amount of law-keeping could make a person right with God. In fact, the law only revealed humanity's sinfulness and inability to live up to God's perfect standard. That's why the message of grace was so revolutionary. It declared that salvation is not about what we do, but about what God has already done for us in Christ. In Ephesians 2:8-9, Paul writes, "For by grace are ye saved through faith; and that not of yourselves: it is the gift of God: Not of works, lest any man should boast." This was the message Paul proclaimed everywhere he went—the Gospel of grace. He wanted people to know that they didn't have to earn God's love or approval; it was already theirs through Jesus. Paul's proclamation of grace was an invitation to rest, to stop striving, and to receive the gift of salvation with open hands.

Paul's role as a proclaimer of God's grace was not without its challenges. Everywhere he went, he faced opposition, both from Jews who clung to the law and from Gentiles who were steeped in paganism. The message of grace was offensive to many—it threatened the religious establishment, it turned the world's values upside down, and it challenged people to let go of their pride and self-reliance. Yet, despite the opposition, Paul never wavered in his mission. He knew that the grace of God was the only hope for a world lost in sin, and he was willing to endure anything to make that message known. In Acts 20:24,

Paul makes it clear that nothing could move him, not even the threat of death. He was willing to lay down his life for the sake of proclaiming the Gospel of grace, because he knew that this message was worth everything. Paul's courage and determination inspire us to ask ourselves if we are willing to proclaim God's grace with the same boldness, even in the face of opposition or hardship. Paul's life teaches us that grace is not just a theological concept—it is the power of God at work in the world, transforming lives, breaking chains of sin, and bringing people into a relationship with the living God.

As a proclaimer of God's grace, Paul also understood the importance of humility. Grace, by its very nature, humbles us. It reminds us that we are not saved because of anything we have done, but solely because of what God has done for us. Paul knew this better than anyone. In 1 Corinthians 15:10, he writes, "But by the grace of God I am what I am: and his grace which was bestowed upon me was not in vain; but I laboured more abundantly than they all: yet not I, but the grace of God which was with me." Paul never took credit for his ministry or his accomplishments. He knew that everything he did, every church he planted, every soul he led to Christ, was the result of God's grace working through him. This humility is at the heart of what it means to proclaim God's grace. When we proclaim grace, we are not pointing people to ourselves; we are pointing them to Jesus, the source of all grace. Paul's life shows us that being a proclaimer of grace means living in complete dependence on God, recognizing that without Him, we can do nothing.

Paul's proclamation of God's grace was also deeply rooted in love. Grace and love go hand in hand, because grace is the expression of God's love toward us. In Romans 5:8, Paul writes, "But God commendeth his love toward us, in that, while we were yet sinners, Christ died for us." This is the heart of the Gospel—the incredible love of God that reaches down to sinners, offering forgiveness, redemption, and new life through Jesus Christ. Paul's proclamation of grace was motivated by love, not only God's love for us but Paul's love for the people he ministered to. He labored tirelessly, enduring hardship, persecution, and suffering, all because he loved the people he was called to serve. In 2 Corinthians 5:14, Paul writes, "For the love of Christ constraineth us." It was the love of Christ that drove Paul to keep going, to keep preaching, to keep proclaiming the message of grace, even when it cost him everything. His life is a powerful example of what it means to be compelled by love, to proclaim

God's grace not out of obligation, but out of a deep, burning desire to see others experience the same love and grace that has transformed our own lives.

As a proclaimer of God's grace, Paul was also deeply concerned with the unity of the church. Grace breaks down barriers, it unites people from every background, every race, and every social class. In Christ, there is no Jew or Gentile, no slave or free, no male or female, but all are one in Him (Galatians 3:28). Paul's proclamation of grace wasn't just about individual salvation; it was about creating a new community, a family of believers who are united in Christ by grace. This is why Paul worked so hard to bring unity to the early church, to break down the walls of division that existed between Jews and Gentiles. He knew that the grace of God had created a new people, a people defined not by their adherence to the law or their ethnic background, but by their faith in Jesus Christ. Paul's life challenges us to think about how we proclaim grace in our own communities. Are we working to break down barriers? Are we proclaiming a message of unity, of inclusion, of love that welcomes all people into the family of God?

Paul's proclamation of God's grace was also deeply hopeful. Grace is the source of our hope because it tells us that our salvation is secure, not because of our efforts, but because of God's faithfulness. In Titus 3:5, Paul writes, "Not by works of righteousness which we have done, but according to his mercy he saved us, by the washing of regeneration, and renewing of the Holy Ghost." This is the hope of grace—that no matter how far we have fallen, no matter how great our sin, God's grace is greater. Paul's message was one of hope for the hopeless, of light for those in darkness. He knew that the grace of God could reach the most hardened heart, the most broken life, and bring healing, restoration, and new life. As a proclaimer of God's grace, Paul was constantly pointing people to the hope of the Gospel, to the promise of eternal life in Christ, to the assurance that God's grace is sufficient for every need.

In conclusion, Paul's role as a proclaimer of God's grace, as described in Acts 20:24, reveals the heart of his ministry and the driving force behind everything he did. Paul's life was consumed with the desire to share the message of grace with the world, to tell everyone about the love of God that is freely given through Jesus Christ. His proclamation of grace was personal, rooted in his own experience of God's mercy. It was radical, challenging the religious and cultural norms of his day. It was humble, recognizing that everything Paul accomplished was by the grace of God. It was motivated by love, driven by a deep desire to see others experience the same grace that had transformed his life. It was a message of unity, breaking down barriers and creating a new community of believers. And it was a message of hope, offering the promise of salvation, forgiveness, and new life to all who would believe. Paul's life as a proclaimer of God's grace continues to inspire and challenge us today, calling us to live lives that reflect the grace we have received and to boldly proclaim the Gospel of grace to a world in desperate need of God's love.

Chapter 17 - Prisoner of Christ

In Philemon 1:9, Paul writes, "Yet for love's sake I rather beseech thee, being such an one as Paul the aged, and now also a prisoner of Jesus Christ." These words are filled with emotion, humility, and the depth of Paul's commitment as a prisoner of Christ, a title that reflects the heart of his identity and ministry. Paul wasn't speaking merely of his physical imprisonment, though at the time he was in chains for preaching the Gospel. No, being a prisoner of Christ went far beyond the walls of any earthly prison. It was a declaration that Paul's entire life was bound to Jesus, that he was willingly captive to Christ's love and mission. To be a prisoner of Christ meant that Paul's freedom, his desires, his plans, and his very life were not his own, but fully surrendered to Jesus. He had been captured by the grace of God, transformed by an encounter with the risen Lord on the road to Damascus, and from that moment forward, he lived as one who was no longer free to live for himself but was joyfully enslaved to the cause of Christ. Paul wore the title of prisoner of Christ as a badge of honor because it signified his total devotion, his complete surrender, and his unbreakable commitment to the one who had saved him.

Paul's use of the term "prisoner of Christ" was rich with meaning, both spiritually and emotionally. It reflected his physical circumstances—he had been arrested multiple times, beaten, imprisoned, and placed in chains for his unshakable faith in Jesus. But even in chains, Paul never considered himself a prisoner of Rome, or of any earthly authority. He understood that he was ultimately a prisoner of Christ, held captive by the love, grace, and call of God. This mindset gave Paul a unique perspective on suffering. He didn't see his imprisonment as a curse or a punishment, but as part of his divine calling. In fact, Paul's imprisonment became a platform for the Gospel. Even in chains, he continued to preach, write letters to the churches, and encourage believers in their faith. His chains didn't limit him; they freed him to rely fully on the power of God. In Philippians 1:12-14, Paul writes, "But I would ye should understand, brethren, that the things which happened unto me have fallen out rather unto the furtherance of the gospel; So that my bonds in Christ are manifest in all the palace, and in all other places; And many of the brethren in the Lord, waxing confident by my bonds, are much more bold to speak the word without fear." Paul's imprisonment, instead of silencing him, amplified his message. He became a living testimony to the power of God's grace and the unshakable nature of the Gospel, which cannot be bound by chains or prison walls.

To be a prisoner of Christ also meant that Paul lived with a profound sense of purpose. He knew that his life was not his own, that he had been "bought with a price" (1 Corinthians 6:20), and that everything he did was for the glory of God. Paul didn't see his circumstances—no matter how difficult or painful—as accidents or misfortunes. He believed that God had a plan for his life, and that even his imprisonment was part of that divine plan. In Romans 8:28, Paul famously wrote, "And we know that all things work together for good to them that love God, to them who are the called according to his purpose." This wasn't just a theological idea for Paul; it was the foundation of his life. As a prisoner of Christ, Paul trusted that God was at work in every situation, using even his chains to advance the Gospel and build up the church. This trust in God's sovereignty gave Paul a sense of peace and joy, even in the most difficult circumstances. He could rejoice in his sufferings because he knew that they were not in vain—they were part of God's larger plan to bring salvation to the world.

Paul's identity as a prisoner of Christ was also deeply connected to his love for the church. Throughout his letters, we see Paul's deep affection for the believers he had led to Christ. He referred to them as his spiritual children, and he carried the weight of their spiritual well-being with him wherever he went. In 2 Corinthians 11:28, Paul writes, "Beside those things that are without, that which cometh upon me daily, the care of all the churches." Even in prison, Paul's heart was with the churches. He wrote letters to encourage, correct, and build them up in their faith. His chains didn't stop him from being a shepherd to the flock of God. In fact, some of Paul's most powerful and influential letters—Ephesians, Philippians, Colossians, and Philemon—were written from prison. These letters are filled with hope, encouragement, and deep theological truths that continue to shape the church today. Paul's imprisonment became an opportunity for him to pour out his heart to the churches, to remind them of the grace of God, and to exhort them to remain steadfast in their faith.

Being a prisoner of Christ also meant that Paul lived with an eternal perspective. He knew that his time on earth was temporary, that the sufferings of this present life were "not worthy to be compared with the glory which shall be revealed in us" (Romans 8:18). This eternal perspective allowed Paul to endure hardships with a sense of joy and hope. He wasn't living for the here and now; he was living for eternity. Paul knew that one day, he would stand before the Lord, and he longed to hear the words, "Well done, thou good and faithful servant" (Matthew 25:21). This future hope gave Paul the strength to persevere through trials, to remain faithful in the face of persecution, and to continue proclaiming the Gospel, even when it cost him everything. As a prisoner of Christ, Paul's life was focused on the eternal, on the kingdom of God, and on the glory that awaited him in the presence of his Savior.

Paul's role as a prisoner of Christ also speaks to the deep humility that characterized his life and ministry. He didn't see himself as a great leader or a powerful apostle, but as a servant of Jesus, willing to go wherever Christ called him, even if that meant suffering and imprisonment. In Philippians 1:21, Paul writes, "For to me to live is Christ, and to die is gain." This statement reflects the depth of Paul's commitment to Christ. Whether in life or in death, Paul's only desire was to glorify Jesus. He didn't cling to his own life or his own comfort; he was willing to give up everything for the sake of the Gospel. This humility, this willingness to be a prisoner of Christ, is a powerful example for all believers. It challenges us to ask ourselves if we are truly willing to surrender everything to Jesus, to follow Him wherever He leads, even if it means suffering, hardship, or loss. Paul's life shows us that true freedom is found not in doing whatever we want, but in surrendering our lives to Christ, in becoming His prisoner, bound by His love and grace.

Paul's identity as a prisoner of Christ also reflects the deep love he had for the people he served. The letter to Philemon, in which Paul calls himself a prisoner of Christ, is a deeply personal and emotional letter. In it, Paul is advocating on behalf of a man named Onesimus, a runaway slave who had become a believer in Christ. Paul appeals to Philemon, Onesimus' master, to receive him back not as a slave but as a beloved brother in Christ. Paul's willingness to intervene on behalf of Onesimus, to advocate for his freedom and reconciliation, shows the depth of his love and commitment to the Gospel of grace. Even as a prisoner, Paul was thinking of others, seeking to bring reconciliation, healing, and unity within the body of Christ. This letter is a beautiful example of how being a prisoner of Christ doesn't mean being focused on oneself, but on serving others with the love of Jesus.

As a prisoner of Christ, Paul's life also reminds us of the power of perseverance. Paul didn't give up when things got hard. He didn't stop preaching the Gospel when he was thrown into prison or when he was beaten and persecuted. In fact, it was in those moments of suffering that Paul's faith shone the brightest. His letters from prison are filled with joy, hope, and encouragement, even though his circumstances were anything but joyful. In Philippians 4:4, Paul writes, "Rejoice in the Lord always: and again I say, Rejoice." These words, written from a prison cell, reflect the depth of Paul's relationship with Christ. His joy wasn't dependent on his circumstances; it was rooted in his relationship with Jesus. Paul's life challenges us to persevere in our own faith, to remain steadfast even in the face of trials, knowing that our hope is in Christ, not in the fleeting comforts of this world.

Paul's identity as a prisoner of Christ also speaks to the power of the Gospel. Paul's chains were a visible reminder of the cost of following Jesus, but they were also a powerful testimony to the freedom that comes from knowing Christ. Even though Paul was physically imprisoned, he was spiritually free. In 2 Timothy 2:9, Paul writes, "Wherein I suffer trouble, as an evil doer, even unto bonds; but the word of God is not bound." Paul knew that no matter how many chains were placed on him, the Gospel could never be chained. The message of salvation through Jesus Christ continued to spread, even while Paul was in prison, because the power of the Gospel is unstoppable. Paul's life shows us that the

message of Christ cannot be silenced, even in the face of persecution. It continues to go forth, bringing life, hope, and salvation to all who believe.

In conclusion, Paul's role as a prisoner of Christ, as described in Philemon 1:9, reveals the depth of his commitment, the strength of his faith, and the love that drove him to continue proclaiming the Gospel, even in the face of suffering. Paul's life as a prisoner of Christ was one of complete surrender to the will of God. He saw himself as a servant of Jesus, willing to endure anything for the sake of the Gospel. His chains didn't limit him; they became a testimony to the power of God's grace and the unshakable nature of the Gospel. Paul's example challenges us to examine our own lives and ask if we are willing to be prisoners of Christ, bound by His love and grace, and committed to His mission no matter the cost. His life reminds us that true freedom is found in surrendering to Jesus, that our joy and hope are not dependent on our circumstances, but on our relationship with Christ. Paul's legacy as a prisoner of Christ continues to inspire and challenge us today, calling us to live lives of faith, perseverance, and love, fully devoted to the one who has captured our hearts with His grace.

Chapter 18 - Disciple of Christ's Sufferings

In 2 Corinthians 11:23-27, Paul gives a gripping account of the sufferings he endured for the sake of the Gospel: "Are they ministers of Christ? (I speak as a fool) I am more; in labours more abundant, in stripes above measure, in prisons more frequent, in deaths oft. Of the Jews five times received I forty stripes save one. Thrice was I beaten with rods, once was I stoned, thrice I suffered shipwreck, a night and a day I have been in the deep; In journeyings often, in perils of waters, in perils of robbers, in perils by mine own countrymen, in perils by the heathen, in perils in the city, in perils in the wilderness, in perils in the sea, in perils among false brethren; In weariness and painfulness, in watchings often, in hunger and thirst, in fastings often, in cold and nakedness." These words give us a glimpse into Paul's role as a disciple of Christ's sufferings, a title that reflects the profound depths of his commitment, sacrifice, and faith. To be a disciple of Christ's sufferings was not merely about enduring pain or hardship for its own sake; it was about following in the footsteps of Jesus, the Suffering Servant, who willingly laid down His life for the salvation of humanity. Paul knew that to follow Christ meant to share in His sufferings, to bear the cross daily, and to endure the trials and tribulations that come with being a servant of the Gospel. His life was marked by suffering, not because he sought it out, but because he was willing to endure whatever was necessary for the sake of Christ and the advancement of the Gospel. Paul's sufferings were a reflection of his deep love for Jesus and his unwavering commitment to the mission of spreading the good news of salvation to the ends of the earth.

Paul's account of his sufferings in 2 Corinthians 11:23-27 is staggering in its detail. He had been beaten, imprisoned, stoned, shipwrecked, and left for dead. He faced danger from every side—robbers, hostile countrymen, false brethren, and natural elements like the sea and wilderness. He knew hunger, thirst, cold, and exhaustion. Yet through it all, Paul never wavered in his faith or his calling. He understood that suffering for the sake of Christ was not something to be avoided but embraced, for it was through suffering that he was being conformed to the image of Christ. In Romans 8:17, Paul writes, "And if children, then heirs; heirs of God, and joint-heirs with Christ; if so be that we suffer with him, that we may be also glorified together." Paul knew that suffering with Christ was not the end of the story—it was the path to glory. His sufferings were not meaningless or purposeless; they were part of the refining process that drew him closer to Jesus and prepared him for the eternal glory that awaited him.

As a disciple of Christ's sufferings, Paul understood that suffering was not a sign of failure or weakness, but a mark of true discipleship. Jesus Himself had warned His followers that they would face persecution and hardship for His name's sake. In John 15:20, Jesus said, "Remember the word that I said unto you, The servant is not greater than his lord. If they have persecuted me, they will also persecute you." Paul knew that to follow Christ was to walk the path of suffering because the world, in its rebellion against God, would always resist the message of the Gospel. But Paul also knew that the sufferings of this present time were nothing compared to the glory that would be revealed in him (Romans 8:18). This hope sustained him through every trial, every beating, and every moment of pain. He knew that his suffering was not in vain—it was producing something far greater than he could see in the moment. In 2 Corinthians 4:17, Paul writes, "For our light affliction, which is but for a moment, worketh for us a far more exceeding and eternal weight of glory." Paul's ability to endure suffering came from his eternal perspective. He wasn't focused on the temporary pain; he was focused on the eternal reward.

Paul's sufferings also deepened his dependence on God. Each trial, each hardship, each moment of pain reminded Paul of his own weakness and God's incredible strength. In 2 Corinthians 12:9-10, Paul shares the lesson he learned through his suffering: "And he said unto me, My grace is sufficient for thee: for my strength is made perfect in weakness. Most gladly therefore will I rather glory in my infirmities, that the power of Christ may rest upon me. Therefore I take pleasure in infirmities, in reproaches, in necessities, in persecutions, in distresses for Christ's sake: for when I am weak, then am I strong." Paul's sufferings stripped away any reliance on his own abilities, forcing him to rely completely on the grace of God. This is one of the most profound lessons of suffering—that in our moments of greatest weakness, God's strength is revealed. Paul didn't just endure suffering; he rejoiced in it, because he knew that through his suffering, the power of Christ was being made manifest in his life. He was a living example of the paradox of the Gospel—that true strength is found in weakness, and true life is found in death to self.

Paul's sufferings also gave him a deeper understanding of Christ's own sufferings. As a disciple of Christ's sufferings, Paul wasn't just suffering for Christ; he was suffering with Christ. In Philippians 3:10, Paul writes, "That I may know him, and the power of his resurrection, and the fellowship of his sufferings, being made conformable unto his death." Paul longed to know Christ more deeply, and he understood that part of that knowing came through sharing in Christ's sufferings. Each beating, each imprisonment, each moment of hardship brought Paul closer to the heart of Jesus, who had suffered and died for the sins of the world. Paul's sufferings were a participation in the sufferings of Christ, a way of entering into the mystery of the cross. This is the deep and beautiful truth of suffering in the Christian life—it is not something to be feared or avoided, but something that, when endured for the sake of Christ, draws us into deeper fellowship with Him. Paul understood this better than anyone, and it was this understanding that gave him the strength to endure.

As a disciple of Christ's sufferings, Paul's life was a powerful testimony to the world. His willingness to endure suffering for the sake of the Gospel showed the world that the message he preached was worth dying for. In a world that values comfort, security, and self-preservation, Paul's life was a radical example of what it means to lay down one's life for Christ. He wasn't interested in personal comfort or safety; he was consumed with the desire to make Christ known, no matter the cost. In Galatians 6:17, Paul writes, "From henceforth let no man trouble me: for I bear in my body the marks of the Lord Jesus." Paul's body literally bore the scars of his suffering for Christ—he had been beaten, whipped, and stoned for the sake of the Gospel. But these scars were not a sign of defeat; they were a testimony to the power of God's grace and the truth of the message Paul proclaimed.

Paul's sufferings also had a profound impact on the church. His willingness to suffer for the sake of Christ inspired others to stand firm in their faith. In Philippians 1:14, Paul writes, "And many of the brethren in the Lord, waxing confident by my bonds, are much more bold to speak the word without fear."

Paul's courage in the face of suffering gave others the strength to proclaim the Gospel with boldness. His life was a living example of what it means to be a disciple of Christ's sufferings, and his testimony continues to inspire believers today to stand firm in their faith, even in the face of persecution.

Paul's role as a disciple of Christ's sufferings also reminds us of the cost of discipleship. Jesus never promised His followers a life of ease or comfort. In fact, He warned that following Him would involve taking up the cross daily and denying oneself (Luke 9:23). Paul understood this better than anyone. He knew that to follow Christ meant to share in His sufferings, but he also knew that the reward of knowing Christ was worth every trial, every hardship, and every moment of pain. Paul's life challenges us to examine our own willingness to suffer for the sake of Christ. Are we willing to endure hardship, persecution, or ridicule for the sake of the Gospel? Are we willing to lay down our own desires, comfort, and security to follow Jesus wherever He leads? Paul's life as a disciple of Christ's sufferings calls us to a deeper level of commitment, a willingness to embrace the cross, knowing that it is through the cross that we find true life.

In conclusion, Paul's role as a disciple of Christ's sufferings, as described in 2 Corinthians 11:23-27, reveals the depth of his commitment to Christ and the Gospel. His life was marked by suffering, but it was also marked by joy, hope, and an unshakable faith in the power of God's grace. Paul's sufferings were not in vain; they were a testimony to the truth of the Gospel and a reflection of his deep love for Jesus. As a disciple of Christ's sufferings, Paul embraced the hardships that came with following Jesus, knowing that through his suffering, he was being conformed to the image of Christ and drawing closer to the heart of his Savior. His life challenges us to embrace our own sufferings, to see them not as obstacles to be avoided, but as opportunities to know Christ more deeply and to participate in the fellowship of His sufferings. Paul's example continues to inspire and challenge believers today, calling us to follow Jesus with the same level of commitment, endurance, and love, no matter the cost.

Chapter 19 - Example of Perseverance

In 2 Timothy 4:7, Paul declares, "I have fought a good fight, I have finished my course, I have kept the faith." These words, written near the end of Paul's life, encapsulate his role as an example of perseverance—a testimony to the endurance, faithfulness, and unwavering commitment that defined his journey with Christ. Paul's life was a long, arduous race, marked by trials, sufferings, and countless challenges, yet he remained steadfast in his mission, his faith, and his love for Jesus. His declaration in this verse is not one of pride or self-congratulation, but of humble satisfaction that he had endured, that he had persevered through every trial, and that he had remained faithful to the call that Christ had placed upon his life. Paul's example of perseverance is a beacon of hope and inspiration for every believer, reminding us that the Christian life is not a sprint but a marathon—a race that requires endurance, courage, and a deep reliance on the grace of God. His words call us to reflect on our own journeys, challenging us to press on, to remain faithful, and to keep our eyes fixed on Jesus, the "author and finisher of our faith" (Hebrews 12:2), knowing that the reward for perseverance is not in this life, but in the eternal life to come.

Paul's life was filled with countless obstacles that could have easily caused him to give up. From the moment he encountered the risen Christ on the road to Damascus, Paul's life was marked by suffering for the sake of the Gospel. He was beaten, imprisoned, shipwrecked, stoned, and left for dead, all because of his commitment to preaching Christ crucified. In 2 Corinthians 11:23-28, Paul gives a staggering account of his sufferings, including receiving thirty-nine lashes on five different occasions, being beaten with rods three times, being shipwrecked three times, and spending a night and a day in the open sea. He faced constant danger from robbers, from his own countrymen, from Gentiles, in the city, in the wilderness, and even among false believers. Yet, despite all these hardships, Paul never wavered. He pressed on, enduring every trial with grace and courage, knowing that his strength came not from himself, but from the Lord. In Philippians 4:13, Paul confidently declares, "I can do all things through Christ which strengtheneth me." Paul's perseverance was not rooted in his own abilities or determination; it was rooted in the grace and power of God that sustained him through every trial. His example reminds us that perseverance is not about never facing difficulties, but about trusting in God's strength to carry us through those difficulties.

Paul's perseverance was fueled by his deep sense of purpose. He knew that he had been called by God to preach the Gospel, to bring the message of salvation to both Jews and Gentiles, and to build up the church. In Acts 20:24, Paul says, "But none of these things move me, neither count I my life dear unto myself, so that I might finish my course with joy, and the ministry, which I have received of the Lord Jesus, to testify the gospel of the grace of God." Paul's singular focus on the mission God had given him kept him moving forward, even when the path was filled with pain and hardship. He didn't allow fear, suffering, or opposition to derail him from his course. He knew that the prize of finishing the race was far greater than any temporary suffering he endured. This sense of purpose gave Paul the strength to keep going when others might have given up. He was running a race, not for earthly rewards, but for an eternal crown. In 1 Corinthians 9:24-25, Paul writes, "Know ye not that they which run in a race run all, but one receiveth the prize? So run, that ye may obtain. And every man that striveth for the mastery is temperate in all things. Now they do it to obtain a corruptible crown; but we an incorruptible." Paul's eyes were fixed on the eternal reward, the incorruptible crown that awaited him at the end of his race. This eternal perspective gave him the strength to persevere, knowing that every trial, every hardship, and every sacrifice was worth it because of the glory that awaited him in the presence of Christ.

Paul's perseverance was also deeply rooted in his love for Christ. He was willing to endure anything because of his love for the Savior who had redeemed him. In Galatians 2:20, Paul writes, "I am crucified with Christ: nevertheless I live; yet not I, but Christ liveth in me: and the life which I now live in the flesh I live by the faith of the Son of God, who loved me, and gave himself for me." Paul's love for Jesus was the driving force behind his perseverance. He knew that Jesus had given His life for him, and in response, Paul was willing to give his life for Jesus. His love for Christ was greater than his fear of suffering or death. This love compelled him to keep going, even when the road was hard, even when the cost was great. Paul's example challenges us to examine the depth of our own love for Christ. Are we willing to persevere through trials and hardships for the sake of the One who gave His life for us? Paul's life reminds us that true perseverance is born out of a deep love for Jesus, a love that is willing to endure anything for His sake.

Paul's example of perseverance also teaches us the importance of faithfulness. In 2 Timothy 4:7, Paul not only says that he has fought a good fight and finished his course, but that he has kept the faith. Throughout his life, Paul remained faithful to the Gospel, to the truth of God's Word, and to the mission God had given him. He didn't compromise, he didn't waver, and he didn't turn away from the truth, even when it would have been easier to do so. In a world filled with false teachings, opposition, and persecution, Paul stood firm in his faith. He held fast to the truth of the Gospel, and he faithfully proclaimed it, even when it cost him everything. Paul's faithfulness in the face of adversity is a powerful example for us today. It reminds us that perseverance is not just about enduring hardship, but about remaining faithful to the truth, to the calling God has placed on our lives, and to the mission of sharing the Gospel with the world. Paul's life calls us to be steadfast in our faith, to hold fast to the truth, and to persevere in proclaiming the Gospel, no matter the cost.

Paul's perseverance was also marked by joy. Despite the many trials he faced, Paul's life was filled with joy because his joy was rooted in Christ. In Philippians 4:4, Paul writes, "Rejoice in the Lord always: and again I say, Rejoice." These words were written while Paul was in prison, yet they reflect the deep, abiding joy that characterized his life. Paul's joy wasn't dependent on his circumstances; it was anchored in his relationship with Jesus. He knew that no matter what trials he faced, nothing could separate him from the love of Christ. This joy gave Paul the strength to keep going, to persevere through every trial with a heart full of praise and thanksgiving. His example teaches us that perseverance is not just about gritting our teeth and pushing through hard times; it's about finding joy in the midst of those trials because we know that Christ is with us, and that He is working all things together for our good. Paul's life reminds us that true joy is found not in the absence of trials, but in the presence of Christ, who walks with us through every storm.

Paul's example of perseverance is also a powerful reminder of the hope we have in Christ. Paul endured so much suffering, but he never lost hope because his hope was anchored in the promises of God. In 2 Timothy 4:8, Paul writes, "Henceforth there is laid up for me a crown of righteousness, which the Lord, the righteous judge, shall give me at that day: and not to me only, but unto all them also that love his appearing." Paul's hope was not in this life, but in the life to come. He knew that at the end of his race, he would receive the crown of righteousness from the Lord. This hope gave Paul the strength to keep going, to persevere through every trial, knowing that his labor was not in vain. Paul's life challenges us to fix our eyes on the eternal hope we have in Christ, to remember that no matter what we face in this life, there is a crown of righteousness waiting for us at the end of our race.

Paul's perseverance was also fueled by his love for the church. Throughout his letters, we see Paul's deep affection for the believers he had led to Christ. He referred to them as his spiritual children, and he labored tirelessly to build them up in their faith, to encourage them, and to help them grow in their relationship with Jesus. In Colossians 1:28-29, Paul writes, "Whom we preach, warning every man, and teaching every man in all wisdom; that we may present every man perfect in Christ Jesus: Whereunto I also labour, striving according to his working, which worketh in me mightily." Paul's perseverance was not just about his own race; it was about helping others run their race as well. He labored and strived to present every believer mature in Christ. His love for the church gave him the strength to keep going, even when the road was hard. Paul's example reminds us that perseverance is not just about our own journey; it's about helping others on their journey as well. We are called to encourage, support, and build up one another in the faith, so that together, we can persevere to the end.

In conclusion, Paul's declaration in 2 Timothy 4:7, "I have fought a good fight, I have finished my course, I have kept the faith," stands as a powerful testimony to his role as an example of perseverance. His life was marked by endurance, faithfulness, and an unwavering commitment to Christ and the Gospel. Through every trial, every hardship, and every moment of suffering, Paul remained steadfast in his faith, his love for Christ, and his mission to proclaim the Gospel. His example challenges us to persevere in our own race, to keep fighting the good fight, to remain faithful to the truth, and to fix our eyes on the eternal reward that awaits us in Christ. Paul's life reminds us that perseverance is not about never facing difficulties, but about trusting in God's strength, finding joy in His presence, and keeping our hope anchored in His promises. As we follow Paul's example of perseverance, we are reminded that the Christian life is a race worth running, and that at the end of the race, there is a crown of righteousness waiting for all who have faithfully endured to the end.

Chapter 20 - Herald of Righteousness by Faith

In Romans 3:22-24, Paul writes, "Even the righteousness of God which is by faith of Jesus Christ unto all and upon all them that believe: for there is no difference: For all have sinned, and come short of the glory of God; Being justified freely by his grace through the redemption that is in Christ Jesus." These words encapsulate Paul's role as a herald of righteousness by faith, a role that defined his entire ministry and shaped his message to the world. In these verses, Paul is proclaiming one of the most foundational and liberating truths of the Gospel: that righteousness—being made right with God—comes not through human effort, not through keeping the law, but through faith in Jesus Christ. This message of righteousness by faith was radical in Paul's time and remains just as powerful today. It declares that salvation is not something we can earn; it is a gift that we receive by faith. Paul understood that humanity, in its sinfulness, could never meet the perfect standard of God's righteousness on its own. That's why the message of grace, of justification through faith, is such incredible news—it levels the playing field for all of us, regardless of our background, our failures, or our attempts to be righteous in our own strength. Through Jesus Christ, God offers a way for sinners to be declared righteous, not by works, but by trusting in what Jesus has already accomplished on the cross. Paul's life was dedicated to heralding this message of righteousness by faith, calling everyone, everywhere, to receive the gift of God's grace and to be reconciled to Him through faith in His Son.

Paul begins in Romans 3:22 by declaring that the righteousness of God comes through faith in Jesus Christ "unto all and upon all them that believe." This is the heart of Paul's Gospel: the good news that righteousness is not reserved for a select few, but is available to everyone who believes. It doesn't matter who you are, where you come from, or what you've done—God's righteousness is offered to all. In a world that often divides people by status, ethnicity, or moral performance, Paul's message was revolutionary. He proclaimed that there is no difference between Jew and Gentile, rich and poor, moral and immoral, because all have sinned and fallen short of the glory of God. No one can claim righteousness on their own, and that's why the Gospel is such good news. It's a message of grace that cuts through the pride of human achievement and levels the ground at the foot of the cross. Paul's declaration that righteousness comes by faith to all who believe shattered the barriers of legalism, self-righteousness, and works-based religion, offering instead the hope of salvation to all who would simply trust in Jesus. This was Paul's calling as a herald of righteousness by faith—to proclaim to the world that God's grace is greater than our sin, and that through faith in Christ, we can stand justified before a holy God.

In Romans 3:23, Paul brings everyone under the same truth: "For all have sinned, and come short of the glory of God." This is the sobering reality that lies at the heart of the Gospel. No one is righteous on their own. Every human being, no matter how good they may appear, has fallen short of God's perfect standard. Paul wasn't afraid to speak the truth about sin, because he knew that until people understood the seriousness of their condition, they would never fully appreciate the magnitude of God's grace. Sin isn't just a minor mistake or a moral failing; it's a rebellion against the holiness of God, and it separates us from Him. Paul's message was clear: all have sinned, and no one can earn their way back to God through their own efforts. But Paul didn't stop at the bad news—he immediately moved to the good news of grace, of righteousness by faith. The very next verse, Romans 3:24, proclaims, "Being justified freely by his grace through the redemption that is in Christ Jesus." This is the heart of the Gospel: though we have all sinned, God has made a way for us to be justified, to be declared righteous, and it comes freely, by His grace. There is nothing we can do to earn it—it is a gift that God offers to all who will receive it by faith.

Paul's role as a herald of righteousness by faith was not just about proclaiming a theological truth; it was about inviting people into a life-changing relationship with God through Jesus Christ. Paul understood that righteousness by faith wasn't just a legal declaration; it was the beginning of a transformed life. When we place our faith in Jesus, we are not only justified—we are made new. Paul himself had experienced this transformation firsthand. Once a persecutor of Christians, driven by self-righteousness and legalism, Paul encountered the risen Christ on the road to Damascus, and his life was never the same. He went from trying to earn his righteousness through the law to receiving it freely by faith in Jesus. His entire ministry was a testimony to the power of God's grace, and his message was simple yet profound: no matter how far you've fallen, no matter how many mistakes you've made, God's grace is sufficient, and through faith in Jesus, you can be made righteous.

Paul's message of righteousness by faith was also a message of hope. For those who had tried and failed to live up to the standards of the law, for those who were burdened by guilt and shame, Paul's proclamation of grace was like water to a parched soul. In Romans 8:1, Paul writes, "There is therefore now no condemnation to them which are in Christ Jesus." This is the promise of righteousness by faith: when we trust in Jesus, we are no longer condemned. Our sins are forgiven, our past is washed clean, and we stand before God clothed in the righteousness of Christ. This was the message Paul heralded to the world—a message of freedom, forgiveness, and new life. It was a message that brought hope to the hopeless, peace to the anxious, and joy to those weighed down by the burden of sin. Paul wanted everyone to know that they didn't have to carry the weight of their sins any longer; they could be justified, made righteous, and reconciled to God through faith in Jesus.

Paul's role as a herald of righteousness by faith was also a role of deep love and compassion. He wasn't preaching a message of condemnation or judgment; he was preaching a message of grace and reconciliation. In 2 Corinthians 5:20, Paul writes, "Now then we are ambassadors for Christ, as though God did beseech you by us: we pray you in Christ's stead, be ye reconciled to God." Paul's heart was to see people reconciled to God, to see them come to a saving knowledge of Jesus Christ and experience the transforming power of His grace. He wasn't interested in winning theological debates or proving himself right; his only goal was to see lives changed by the Gospel. Paul's message of righteousness by faith wasn't just about what happens after we die; it was about the new life that begins the moment we place our faith in Jesus. Paul knew that the grace of God had the power to transform hearts, to break the chains of sin, and to bring people into a relationship with God that would change everything. His proclamation of righteousness by faith was an invitation to experience the fullness of God's love and grace, to step out of the darkness of sin and into the light of His righteousness.

Paul's message of righteousness by faith was also a message of unity. In a world divided by ethnicity, social status, and religious background, Paul's proclamation that righteousness comes by faith alone, to all who believe, broke down the barriers that separated people from one another. In Galatians 3:28, Paul writes, "There is neither Jew nor Greek, there is neither bond nor free, there is neither male nor female: for ye are all one in Christ Jesus." This is the power of righteousness by faith—it unites us all under the banner of Christ. Whether Jew or Gentile, rich or poor, male or female, we all come to God on the same terms: by grace, through faith. There is no hierarchy in the Kingdom of God, no one who is more deserving of righteousness than another. Paul's message of righteousness by faith was a call to unity, to recognize that we are all equally in need of God's grace, and that through faith in Jesus, we are all made one in Him.

Paul's proclamation of righteousness by faith was also a message of freedom. In Romans 6:14, Paul writes, "For sin shall not have dominion over you: for ye are not under the law, but under grace." This is the freedom that comes from righteousness by faith—freedom from the power of sin, freedom from the burden of the law, and freedom to live a new life in Christ. Paul understood that the law, while good and holy, could never save. It could only reveal our sin and our need for a Savior. But through faith in Jesus, we are no longer under the law's condemnation; we are under grace. This grace doesn't just forgive us; it empowers us to live a life of righteousness. Paul's message wasn't just about being declared righteous; it was about being transformed by the grace of God into people who live righteously, not because we are trying to earn God's favor, but because we have already received it.

In conclusion, Paul's role as a herald of righteousness by faith, as described in Romans 3:22-24, was the defining mission of his life. His message was clear: righteousness comes not by works, not by keeping the law, but by faith in Jesus Christ. It is a gift of grace, freely given to all who believe, and it is available to everyone, regardless of who they are or what they have done. Paul's proclamation of righteousness by faith was a message of hope, freedom, and transformation—a message that continues to resonate today. His life and ministry were a testament to the power of God's grace, and his words continue to call people to faith in Jesus, to receive the gift of righteousness, and to live in the freedom and joy that comes from being justified by grace through faith. As a herald of righteousness by faith, Paul invites us all to lay down our attempts to earn God's favor and to receive, by faith, the righteousness that comes only through Jesus Christ. His message is one of love, grace, and unity, and it challenges us to live in the light of God's grace, knowing that we are justified freely through the redemption that is in Christ Jesus.

Chapter 21 - Revealer of the Mystery of Christ

In Ephesians 3:3-5, Paul writes, "How that by revelation he made known unto me the mystery; (as I wrote afore in few words, Whereby, when ye read, ye may understand my knowledge in the mystery of Christ) Which in other ages was not made known unto the sons of men, as it is now revealed unto his holy apostles and prophets by the Spirit." These verses capture Paul's extraordinary role as the Revealer of the Mystery of Christ, a title that reflects his God-given responsibility to unveil the profound truths of the Gospel that had been hidden for ages but were now made known through Jesus Christ. The "mystery" that Paul refers to is not a puzzle or a secret to be solved by human intellect; it is a divine truth that had been concealed in the mind of God for generations, only to be revealed at the appointed time through Christ and made known by the Spirit to Paul and the apostles. This mystery, which Paul tirelessly preached, was the stunning revelation that God's plan of salvation was not limited to the Jewish people alone, but extended to the Gentiles as well. Through Jesus Christ, the wall of division between Jew and Gentile had been torn down, and now all people, regardless of background, ethnicity, or nationality, could come to God and be part of His family by faith. The mystery that Paul revealed was the glorious truth that in Christ, all people are made one—co-heirs, members of the same body, and sharers in the promise of salvation. This truth was revolutionary in Paul's time and remains just as transformative today. His life as the revealer of the mystery of Christ was a life devoted to proclaiming the inclusivity of God's grace and the breathtaking scope of His redemptive plan for humanity.

Paul's revelation of the mystery of Christ wasn't something he discovered on his own; it was given to him by direct revelation from God. In Galatians 1:11-12, Paul writes, "But I certify you, brethren, that the gospel which was preached of me is not after man. For I neither received it of man, neither was I taught it, but by the revelation of Jesus Christ." This divine revelation was what set Paul's ministry apart—he wasn't preaching a message he had been taught by human teachers or one that was based on the traditions of men. He was declaring the very truth of God, revealed to him by the Holy Spirit, that had been hidden in ages past but was now made known in Christ. Paul's role as the revealer of the mystery of Christ gave him a profound sense of responsibility. He wasn't just sharing an interesting theological idea; he was unveiling the very heart of God's plan for the redemption of the world. The mystery that Paul proclaimed was the culmination of God's work throughout history, from the promises made to Abraham to the coming of the Messiah, Jesus. It was the fulfillment of God's covenant, and it was a message that changed everything.

At the center of this mystery was the truth that through Christ, God was reconciling not only the Jewish people but all humanity to Himself. In Ephesians 2:14, Paul declares, "For he is our peace, who hath made both one, and hath broken down the middle wall of partition between us." This was the crux of the mystery: the barrier between Jew and Gentile, which had stood for centuries, had been broken down by Jesus' death and resurrection. No longer were the Gentiles considered outsiders or strangers to God's covenant promises. Through Christ, they were brought near, made part of the same body, and given access to the same promises. This was a radical message in Paul's time, especially to the Jewish community, who had long believed that they alone were God's chosen people. But Paul, as the revealer of the mystery of Christ, boldly proclaimed that in Christ, there was no longer any division. All who put their faith in Jesus were part of the same family, united by the Spirit and equal before God.

Paul's role as the revealer of the mystery of Christ was not just about doctrinal truth; it was about a new way of living and being in the world. The mystery that he unveiled had profound implications for how believers related to one another and to the world around them. No longer could they see themselves as divided by race, culture, or background. In Galatians 3:28, Paul writes, "There is neither Jew nor Greek, there is neither bond nor free, there is neither male nor female: for ye are all one in Christ Jesus." This was the revolutionary nature of the mystery of Christ—it created a new humanity, one that transcended the divisions of the past and united all believers in the body of Christ. Paul's message wasn't just about individual salvation; it was about the creation of a new community, a new people who were called to live in unity, love, and peace, reflecting the reconciling power of the Gospel to the world. This was the mystery that had been hidden but was now revealed: that through Christ, God was creating a new humanity, a new family made up of people from every nation, tribe, and tongue, united by faith in Jesus.

As the revealer of the mystery of Christ, Paul was driven by a deep sense of urgency and passion. He knew that this revelation wasn't something to be kept hidden or confined to a select few; it was a message that needed to be proclaimed to the ends of the earth. In Romans 1:16, Paul boldly declares, "For I am not ashamed of the gospel of Christ: for it is the power of God unto salvation to every one that believeth; to the Jew first, and also to the Greek." Paul's heart burned with the desire to make known the mystery of Christ to everyone, both Jew and Gentile, so that all people could come to know the salvation that is found in Jesus. He traveled tirelessly, endured countless hardships, and faced fierce opposition, all for the sake of proclaiming the mystery of Christ. He knew that this message had the power to transform lives, to bring hope to the hopeless, and to reconcile humanity to God. Paul's life as the revealer of the mystery of Christ was a life lived with singular focus and unwavering determination to make known the riches of God's grace to all who would listen.

Paul's revelation of the mystery of Christ also carried with it a message of deep hope. The mystery wasn't just about bringing people together; it was about revealing the ultimate purpose of God's redemptive plan. In Ephesians 1:9-10, Paul writes, "Having made known unto us the mystery of his will, according to his good pleasure which he hath purposed in himself: That in the dispensation of the fulness of times he might gather together in one all things in Christ, both which are in heaven, and which are on earth; even in him." The mystery of Christ is the revelation that God is in the process of restoring and reconciling all things to Himself through Jesus. This isn't just about individual salvation—it's about the cosmic scope of God's redemptive plan. Through Christ, God is bringing healing, restoration, and reconciliation to the entire created order. This is the ultimate hope of the Gospel, and it's a hope that Paul eagerly proclaimed as the revealer of this mystery. Paul's life and message were filled with the hope that one day, all things would be made new in Christ, and that the divisions, pain, and brokenness of this world would be healed by the power of God's grace.

As the revealer of the mystery of Christ, Paul's message also carried with it the call to mission. He knew that the revelation of this mystery wasn't something to be kept to a small group of believers; it was a message that needed to be shared with the entire world. In Ephesians 3:8, Paul writes, "Unto me, who am less than the least of all saints, is this grace given, that I should preach among the Gentiles the unsearchable riches of Christ." Paul understood that the mystery of Christ wasn't just for the Jewish people—it was for the Gentiles, for the nations, for all who would believe. His life was dedicated to making this mystery known, traveling from city to city, preaching the Gospel, and planting churches. Paul's revelation of the mystery of Christ was inseparable from his sense of mission. He believed that every person, no matter their background, had the right to hear the good news of Jesus and to respond to God's invitation to be part of His family. This is the mission that continues to drive the church today—to make known the mystery of Christ to a world that desperately needs to hear the message of God's grace.

In conclusion, Paul's role as the Revealer of the Mystery of Christ, as described in Ephesians 3:3-5, was central to his calling and ministry. He was entrusted with the divine revelation that had been hidden for ages but was now made known in Christ—the glorious truth that through Jesus, all people, Jew and Gentile alike, are reconciled to God and made part of His family. Paul's life was dedicated to proclaiming this mystery, to making known the riches of God's grace, and to inviting all people to come and be part of the new humanity that God was creating through Christ. His message was one of unity, hope, and mission, calling believers to live in the light of the Gospel and to share the good news of God's grace with the world. As the revealer of the mystery of Christ, Paul's life and ministry continue to inspire and challenge us today, reminding us of the incredible privilege we have to know and proclaim the mystery of Christ and to invite others into the life-transforming grace of God.

Chapter 22 - Spiritual Warrior

In Ephesians 6:12-13, Paul writes, "For we wrestle not against flesh and blood, but against principalities, against powers, against the rulers of the darkness of this world, against spiritual wickedness in high places. Wherefore take unto you the whole armour of God, that ye may be able to withstand in the evil day, and having done all, to stand." These verses reveal Paul's role as a spiritual warrior, calling all believers to recognize that the Christian life is not just a peaceful journey but a constant battle against spiritual forces of darkness. Paul's message here is a call to arms—not against people or earthly powers, but against the invisible, powerful forces of evil that seek to oppose God's kingdom and derail our faith. As a spiritual warrior, Paul understood that this battle is real and ongoing, and it requires strength, vigilance, and, most importantly, the power of God. In this passage, Paul opens the eyes of the church to the reality of the spiritual warfare that surrounds us and urges us to be fully prepared for the fight. The enemies we face are not physical; they are spiritual—forces that operate in the unseen realm, influencing the world with sin, deception, and destruction. But Paul's message is not one of fear; it is one of hope, because God has provided us with everything we need to stand firm and be victorious in this battle. The "whole armour of God" is not just a metaphor—it is a spiritual reality, a divine provision that equips us to fight the good fight of faith, to resist the attacks of the enemy, and to stand strong in the face of evil.

Paul's role as a spiritual warrior wasn't just theoretical; it was born out of his own experiences. Throughout his life, Paul encountered intense spiritual opposition as he preached the Gospel and advanced God's kingdom. From the moment of his conversion on the road to Damascus, Paul became a target of the enemy, who sought to stop him from fulfilling his mission. He was imprisoned, beaten, shipwrecked, stoned, and faced countless other hardships, yet through it all, Paul never wavered in his faith or his commitment to the cause of Christ.

He knew that the opposition he faced wasn't just from human enemies, but from spiritual forces working behind the scenes to try and stop the spread of the Gospel. Paul was intimately familiar with the reality of spiritual warfare, and he understood that the only way to withstand these attacks was to rely on God's strength and to be fully armed with His spiritual armor. Paul's life as a spiritual warrior serves as an example for all believers of what it means to stand firm in the midst of spiritual battles, trusting not in our own strength, but in the power of God.

In Ephesians 6:12, Paul explains that our struggle is not "against flesh and blood"—in other words, the battle we are engaged in is not against other people. This is a critical point for every believer to understand, because it can be easy to think that our enemies are those who oppose us, those who mock our faith, or those who spread evil in the world. But Paul makes it clear that the true enemy is not human; it is spiritual. The forces we are fighting against are "principalities," "powers," "rulers of the darkness of this world," and "spiritual wickedness in high places." These are descriptions of the hierarchy of demonic forces that operate in the spiritual realm. These forces seek to deceive, destroy, and lead people away from God. They operate through lies, temptation, and fear, and their goal is to prevent people from coming to the knowledge of the truth and to hinder the work of God's kingdom. Paul knew that the stakes in this battle were high, because it is a battle for the souls of men and women. As a spiritual warrior, Paul was deeply aware of the enemy's tactics, but he also knew that in Christ, we have the victory. His message to the Ephesians was meant to open their eyes to the reality of this battle and to equip them with the tools they needed to fight effectively.

Paul's call to take up "the whole armour of God" in Ephesians 6:13 is a rallying cry for all believers to be fully prepared for the spiritual battles we face. The armor of God is not just a defensive measure; it is also a source of strength and confidence. Paul knew that no soldier would go into battle without being fully equipped, and the same is true for Christians in spiritual warfare. The armor of God includes the belt of truth, the breastplate of righteousness, the shoes of the Gospel of peace, the shield of faith, the helmet of salvation, and the sword of the Spirit, which is the Word of God. Each piece of armor represents a vital aspect of the believer's defense against the enemy's attacks. The belt of truth reminds us that we stand on the truth of God's Word, and that truth holds everything else together. The breastplate of righteousness protects our hearts, reminding us that we are righteous in Christ, not because of our own works, but because of His grace. The shoes of the Gospel of peace equip us to stand firm and to advance the message of the Gospel, even in the midst of conflict. The shield of faith extinguishes the fiery darts of the enemy—doubts, lies, and accusations that seek to undermine our confidence in God. The helmet of salvation guards our minds, reminding us that we are saved and secure in Christ. And the sword of the Spirit, the Word of God, is our offensive weapon, enabling us to counter the enemy's lies with the truth of Scripture.

Paul's description of the armor of God emphasizes the fact that spiritual warfare is not something we can engage in with our own strength or resources. We need God's armor because the battle is too great for us to fight on our own. As a spiritual warrior, Paul understood that victory in this battle comes not from relying on human wisdom or strength, but from standing firm in the power of God and using the spiritual weapons He has given us. In 2 Corinthians 10:4, Paul writes, "For the weapons of our warfare are not carnal, but mighty through God to the pulling down of strong holds." Paul knew that the only way to defeat the forces of darkness was through the mighty power of God, and that power is made available to every believer who takes up the armor of God and fights in His strength.

As a spiritual warrior, Paul also understood the importance of prayer in the midst of battle. In Ephesians 6:18, immediately after describing the armor of God, Paul writes, "Praying always with all prayer and supplication in the Spirit, and watching thereunto with all perseverance and supplication for all saints." Prayer is the lifeblood of the spiritual warrior. It is through prayer that we stay connected to God's power, receive His guidance, and remain vigilant against the enemy's attacks. Paul knew that no battle could be fought or won without constant communication with the Commander of the army—Jesus Christ. Prayer is not just a defensive tool; it is a powerful weapon that can tear down strongholds, break chains, and open the way for God's kingdom to advance. As a spiritual warrior, Paul relied on prayer for strength, wisdom, and endurance, and he urged the church to do the same. His life was a testament to the power of prayer, and he knew that it was through prayer that believers would be able to stand firm in the evil day and resist the attacks of the enemy.

Paul's role as a spiritual warrior also involved training and equipping others for the battle. Throughout his letters, we see Paul encouraging and exhorting believers to be strong in the Lord, to stand firm in their faith, and to be vigilant against the enemy's schemes. In 1 Corinthians 16:13, Paul writes, "Watch ye, stand fast in the faith, quit you like men, be strong." Paul knew that the battle was not just his to fight; every believer is called to be a soldier in God's army, and every believer must be equipped for the fight. Paul's life as a spiritual warrior was not just about his own personal battles; it was about raising up an army of believers who were strong in the Lord, who knew how to put on the armor of God, and who were ready to fight the good fight of faith. His letters are filled with encouragement, exhortation, and instruction, all designed to equip the church for the spiritual warfare they would face. Paul was not content to fight alone; he was passionate about training others to stand strong in the Lord and to be victorious in the spiritual battles they would encounter.

As a spiritual warrior, Paul also understood that the battle was already won in Christ. While the warfare is real and the enemy is powerful, Paul knew that Jesus had already secured the ultimate victory through His death and resurrection. In Colossians 2:15, Paul writes, "And having spoiled principalities and powers, he made a shew of them openly, triumphing over them in it." Jesus has already defeated the forces of darkness, and as believers, we fight from a place of victory, not defeat. Paul's role as a spiritual warrior was not about striving to win a battle that was still undecided; it was about standing firm in the victory that Christ has already won. This is the great hope and confidence that we have as spiritual warriors—we are fighting a defeated enemy, and the power of Christ is greater than anything the enemy can throw at us. Paul's life and message remind us that we are more than conquerors through Him who loved us (Romans 8:37), and that no weapon formed against us will prosper (Isaiah 54:17).

In conclusion, Paul's role as a spiritual warrior, as described in Ephesians 6:12-13, was central to his life and ministry. He understood that the Christian life is a battle, not against flesh and blood, but against spiritual forces of darkness that seek to oppose God's kingdom and destroy our faith. As a spiritual warrior, Paul fought not with physical weapons, but with the whole armor of God, relying on God's strength, prayer, and the power of His Word. His life was a testament to the reality of spiritual warfare, and he called the church to be fully equipped for the fight, standing firm in the victory that Christ has already won. Paul's example challenges us to take up the armor of God, to be vigilant in prayer, and to stand strong in the face of spiritual opposition, knowing that we fight from a place of victory and that, through Christ, we are more than conquerors. His life as a spiritual warrior continues to inspire and equip believers today to engage in the battle, trusting in the power of God to overcome every force of darkness and to bring His kingdom to earth.

Chapter 23 - Shepherd of the Flock

In Acts 20:28, Paul addresses the elders of the church in Ephesus with these words: "Take heed therefore unto yourselves, and to all the flock, over the which the Holy Ghost hath made you overseers, to feed the church of God, which he hath purchased with his own blood." This powerful verse highlights Paul's role as a Shepherd of the Flock, a role that not only reflects his deep care for the churches he established but also his profound understanding of the responsibility and love that a shepherd must have for his sheep. Paul, like a shepherd, was called to care for, protect, nurture, and lead the flock of God, the people for whom Christ had given His life. In this passage, we see Paul, at the end of his ministry in Ephesus, giving a solemn charge to the leaders of the church to take up the mantle of shepherding with the same dedication and vigilance that he himself had shown. His words, inspired by the Holy Spirit, remind us that the church is precious to God—so precious that He purchased it with the blood of His own Son. This truth imbues the role of the shepherd with an immense sense of gravity and urgency. The shepherd is not merely a leader or teacher; he is a caretaker of souls, entrusted with the spiritual well-being of God's people, and Paul embodied this responsibility with unwavering devotion throughout his ministry.

Paul's heart as a shepherd was evident in the way he poured out his life for the sake of the flock. He traveled extensively, endured persecution, faced imprisonment, and suffered numerous hardships, all because of his deep love for the people of God. Like a shepherd who tirelessly watches over his sheep, Paul was relentless in his care for the church. He knew that the church was not a building or an institution, but a living body of believers—people who needed guidance, encouragement, protection, and spiritual nourishment. In 1 Thessalonians 2:7-8, Paul describes his approach to ministry, saying, "But we were gentle among you, even as a nurse cherisheth her children: So being affectionately desirous of you, we were willing to have imparted unto you, not the gospel of God only, but also our own souls, because ye were dear unto us." Paul's shepherding was not impersonal or distant; it was marked by deep, personal involvement in the lives of the believers. He didn't just preach to them; he loved them, prayed for them, wept with them, and shared in their joys and sorrows. His heart was completely invested in their spiritual growth, and he longed to see them mature in Christ, fully equipped to stand firm in their faith.

In Acts 20:28, Paul emphasizes that the flock belongs to God, not to the shepherds. The church is "the church of God, which he hath purchased with his own blood." This statement underscores the profound value and worth of every believer in God's sight. The church is not something to be taken lightly; it is a community of people redeemed at the highest cost—the blood of Jesus Christ. Paul's understanding of this truth shaped his entire approach to shepherding. He knew that the people he was called to lead and care for were not his own; they belonged to God, and he was merely a steward of the flock. This awareness filled Paul with a deep sense of responsibility, knowing that he would one day have to give an account to God for how he cared for His people. Paul's example challenges every spiritual leader to approach their role with humility, reverence, and a deep sense of the sacred trust they have been given. The flock is not ours; it is God's, and we are called to care for it with the same love and devotion that Christ Himself showed when He laid down His life for the sheep.

Paul's role as a shepherd was not without challenges. He faced opposition from false teachers, persecution from authorities, and even division within the church itself. Yet through it all, Paul remained steadfast in his commitment to the flock. He warned the Ephesian elders in Acts 20:29-30, saying, "For I know this, that after my departing shall grievous wolves enter in among you, not sparing the flock. Also of your own selves shall men arise, speaking perverse things, to draw away disciples after them." Paul understood the dangers that the church would face, both from external threats and from internal divisions. He knew that false teachers would try to lead the believers astray and that wolves would come in, seeking to destroy the flock. As a shepherd, Paul was vigilant, always on guard against these threats, and he urged the leaders of the church to do the same. His life was a constant battle to protect the flock from spiritual danger, and he was willing to confront false teachings, correct wrong behavior, and stand up to those who sought to harm the church, all because of his deep love for the people of God.

Paul's care for the flock wasn't just about protecting them from danger; it was also about feeding them spiritually. In Acts 20:28, he exhorts the elders to "feed the church of God." The role of the shepherd is to provide spiritual nourishment for the flock, to ensure that they are growing in their faith and knowledge of God. Paul knew that the church needed sound teaching, rooted in the truth of the Gospel, in order to grow strong and mature in their faith. He devoted himself to preaching and teaching the Word of God, both publicly and privately, ensuring that the believers were grounded in the truth. In 2 Timothy 4:2, Paul charges Timothy to "preach the word; be instant in season, out of season; reprove, rebuke, exhort with all longsuffering and doctrine." Paul's life as a shepherd was marked by a relentless commitment to the Word of God, knowing that it was the only source of spiritual life and growth for the church. His example challenges every spiritual leader to prioritize the teaching and preaching of the Word, to feed the flock with the nourishment that comes from Scripture, and to ensure that the church is growing in its understanding of the Gospel.

As a shepherd, Paul also modeled the importance of leading by example. In 1 Corinthians 11:1, he writes, "Be ye followers of me, even as I also am of Christ." Paul didn't just tell the believers how to live; he showed them through his own life. He lived out the Gospel in every aspect of his life, demonstrating what it meant to follow Christ with humility, perseverance, and faithfulness. Paul's life was a living sermon, and he understood that as a shepherd, his actions spoke as loudly as his words. He wasn't afraid to share his struggles, his weaknesses, or his failures with the church, because he knew that authenticity and transparency were key to effective shepherding. Paul's example reminds us that spiritual leadership is not about perfection, but about faithfully following Christ and leading others to do the same. His life challenges every shepherd to lead with integrity, to live in a way that reflects the love and holiness of Christ, and to be an example for the flock to follow.

Paul's role as a shepherd was also deeply relational. He didn't see the church as an organization to manage, but as a family to love and care for. In 1 Thessalonians 2:11-12, Paul writes, "As ye know how we exhorted and comforted and charged every one of you, as a father doth his children, That ye would walk worthy of God, who hath called you unto his kingdom and glory." Paul's approach to shepherding was like that of a father caring for his children—full of love, tenderness, and encouragement. He wasn't distant or detached from the believers; he was intimately involved in their lives, sharing in their struggles, offering comfort in their trials, and urging them to walk faithfully with God. His shepherding was marked by a deep, personal investment in the lives of the people he led. He didn't just care about their spiritual growth; he cared about their whole being—their joys, their sorrows, their challenges, and their victories. Paul's life as a shepherd challenges us to remember that shepherding is not just about preaching sermons or leading programs; it's about loving people, walking with them through the ups and downs of life, and helping them grow in their relationship with Christ.

In conclusion, Paul's role as a Shepherd of the Flock, as described in Acts 20:28, was central to his life and ministry. He understood the sacred responsibility of caring for the church of God, knowing that it had been purchased with the precious blood of Christ. Paul's heart as a shepherd was filled with love, compassion, and a deep sense of responsibility for the spiritual well-being of the believers. He protected the flock from spiritual danger, fed them with the nourishment of God's Word, and led them by example, showing them what it meant to follow Christ. His life as a shepherd was not about authority or power; it was about sacrificial love, humble service, and a deep commitment to the people of God. Paul's example continues to inspire and challenge us today, reminding us of the importance of shepherding the flock with the same love, care, and devotion that Christ showed when He laid down His life for the sheep. As shepherds of the flock, we are called to love, protect, feed, and lead God's people, always mindful of the great responsibility we have been given and the immeasurable value of the flock that has been entrusted to our care.

Chapter 24 - Champion of Christian Liberty

In Galatians 5:1, Paul writes, "Stand fast therefore in the liberty wherewith Christ hath made us free, and be not entangled again with the yoke of bondage." These powerful words capture Paul's role as a Champion of Christian Liberty, a title that reflects his fierce commitment to the truth that through Christ, believers have been set free from the chains of sin, the condemnation of the law, and the oppressive weight of legalism. Paul's entire life and ministry were dedicated to proclaiming the freedom that is found in Jesus Christ, and he passionately fought against any teaching or practice that sought to bring believers back into bondage. To Paul, Christian liberty was not just a theological concept—it was the very heartbeat of the Gospel, the glorious reality that through faith in Christ, we are no longer slaves to sin or bound by the impossible demands of the law. Instead, we are free to live in the grace of God, empowered by the Holy Spirit to walk in righteousness, love, and joy. This freedom is not something that can be earned; it is a gift that comes through the finished work of Jesus on the cross. Paul's declaration in Galatians 5:1 is both a reminder and a command for believers to stand firm in this liberty, to hold fast to the freedom that Christ has given, and to resist any attempt to return to the bondage of legalism or works-based righteousness. Paul's role as the champion of Christian liberty was marked by his unwavering commitment to ensuring that the church understood, embraced, and lived out the freedom that is found in Christ.

Paul's proclamation of Christian liberty was rooted in his own profound experience of grace. Before his encounter with the risen Christ on the road to Damascus, Paul was a zealous Pharisee, deeply committed to the law and to the idea that righteousness could be attained through strict adherence to religious rules and regulations. He was, in his own words, "a Hebrew of the Hebrews; as touching the law, a Pharisee" (Philippians 3:5). But when Paul met Jesus, everything changed. In that moment, Paul realized that all of his efforts to earn righteousness through the law were worthless compared to the surpassing worth of knowing Christ and being found in Him. In Philippians 3:9, Paul writes, "And be found in him, not having mine own righteousness, which is of the law, but that which is through the faith of Christ, the righteousness which is of God by faith." This revelation transformed Paul's entire life and ministry. He understood that righteousness is not something we can achieve through our own efforts; it is a gift that is received by faith in Jesus Christ. This understanding of grace became the foundation of Paul's message of Christian liberty, and he became its most passionate defender, determined to ensure that no believer would ever fall back into the bondage of trying to earn God's favor through the law.

In Galatians 5:1, Paul commands the believers to "stand fast" in the liberty that Christ has given them. This phrase "stand fast" is a call to action—it's a military term that conveys the idea of holding your ground, of standing firm in the face of opposition. Paul knew that the liberty we have in Christ is something that must be protected, because there will always be forces that seek to undermine it. In the context of the Galatian church, false teachers known as Judaizers had infiltrated the church, teaching that in order to be truly righteous, believers needed to follow certain Jewish laws, such as circumcision. These false teachers were trying to convince the Galatians that faith in Christ wasn't enough—they needed to add works of the law to their faith in order to be fully accepted by God. Paul saw this teaching for what it was—a direct assault on the Gospel of grace and a dangerous attempt to bring believers back into the bondage of legalism. That's why he wrote the letter to the Galatians with such urgency and passion, warning them not to be "entangled again with the yoke of bondage." Paul knew that once you start relying on your own works to earn God's favor, you are no longer living in the freedom that Christ has given—you are putting yourself back under the weight of the law, which can only lead to frustration, guilt, and spiritual defeat.

Paul's defense of Christian liberty was not just about rejecting legalism; it was about embracing the full reality of what Christ has accomplished for us. Through His death and resurrection, Jesus has set us free from the power of sin, the condemnation of the law, and the fear of judgment. In Romans 8:1, Paul writes, "There is therefore now no condemnation to them which are in Christ

Jesus, who walk not after the flesh, but after the Spirit." This is the essence of Christian liberty—freedom from condemnation, freedom from the impossible burden of trying to earn our way to God, and freedom to live in the grace, peace, and love of Christ. Paul wanted the Galatians to understand that they were no longer slaves; they were sons and daughters of God, adopted into His family and given the Spirit of God to lead and guide them. In Galatians 4:6-7, Paul writes, "And because ye are sons, God hath sent forth the Spirit of his Son into your hearts, crying, Abba, Father. Wherefore thou art no more a servant, but a son; and if a son, then an heir of God through Christ." This is the freedom that Paul was fighting for—the freedom of knowing that we are fully accepted by God, not because of what we have done, but because of what Christ has done for us. This freedom changes everything. It sets us free from the fear of failure, the need to prove ourselves, and the burden of trying to earn God's love. In Christ, we are already loved, already accepted, and already made righteous by faith.

But Paul also understood that Christian liberty is not a license to live however we want. In Galatians 5:13, he writes, "For, brethren, ye have been called unto liberty; only use not liberty for an occasion to the flesh, but by love serve one another." True Christian liberty is not about indulging our sinful desires or living without any moral restraint. It is about being set free from sin so that we can live in the power of the Spirit and serve others in love. Paul knew that there was a danger in misunderstanding liberty as freedom to do whatever we please, and he was careful to clarify that the liberty we have in Christ is a freedom to live in righteousness, to walk in the Spirit, and to love others as Christ has loved us. Christian liberty is not self-centered; it is Christ-centered. It is the freedom to live the life God has called us to live, empowered by His grace and guided by His Spirit. Paul's role as a champion of Christian liberty was not just about setting people free from legalism; it was about calling them to a higher way of living—a life of love, service, and holiness that flows from the freedom we have in Christ.

Paul's message of Christian liberty was deeply personal for him. He had experienced the crushing weight of legalism firsthand, and he knew the joy and freedom that came from being set free by the grace of God. In Philippians 3:7-8, Paul writes, "But what things were gain to me, those I counted loss for Christ. Yea doubtless, and I count all things but loss for the excellency of the knowledge of Christ Jesus my Lord: for whom I have suffered the loss of all things, and do count them but dung, that I may win Christ." Paul had once prided himself on his religious achievements, but after encountering Christ, he realized that all of his efforts to earn righteousness were worthless. He found true freedom, not in the law, but in knowing Christ and being found in Him. This personal experience of grace fueled Paul's passion to proclaim Christian liberty to others. He didn't want anyone to live under the bondage of legalism or works-based righteousness. He wanted every believer to experience the same freedom he had found in Christ—the freedom to live in the joy, peace, and love of God, knowing that they were fully accepted by Him through faith.

Paul's role as a champion of Christian liberty also involved standing up against those who sought to impose legalism on the church. In Galatians 2:4-5, Paul recounts how certain false brethren had "privily brought in" false teachings, trying to "spy out our liberty which we have in Christ Jesus, that they might bring us into bondage." But Paul refused to give in to their demands, saying, "To whom we gave place by subjection, no, not for an hour; that the truth of the gospel might continue with you." Paul was willing to stand up and fight for the truth of Christian liberty, even when it meant confronting influential leaders or enduring persecution. He knew that the Gospel of grace was at stake, and he was determined to protect the freedom that Christ had won for His people. Paul's courage in defending Christian liberty challenges us to do the same. We, too, must be vigilant in standing against any teaching or practice that seeks to undermine the freedom we have in Christ, and we must be willing to stand firm in the truth of the Gospel, no matter the cost.

In conclusion, Paul's role as a Champion of Christian Liberty, as described in Galatians 5:1, was central to his life and ministry. He understood that through Christ, we have been set free from the bondage of sin, the condemnation of the law, and the weight of legalism, and he fought tirelessly to ensure that the church lived in the full reality of that freedom. Paul's message of Christian liberty was not just about rejecting legalism; it was about embracing the grace of God, walking in the power of the Spirit, and living a life of love and service. His life and ministry were a testimony to the transforming power of God's grace, and his words continue to inspire and challenge us today to stand firm in the liberty that Christ has given us, to resist any attempt to return to bondage, and to live in the freedom, joy, and peace of knowing that we are fully accepted by God through faith in Jesus Christ. As a champion of Christian liberty, Paul calls us to live in the freedom that Christ has won for us, to walk in the Spirit, and to love and serve one another in the grace and power of God.

Chapter 25 - Builder on Christ, the Foundation

In 1 Corinthians 3:11, Paul writes, "For other foundation can no man lay than that is laid, which is Jesus Christ." These words reveal Paul's role as a Builder on Christ, the Foundation, a title that speaks to his tireless work in establishing churches, spreading the Gospel, and ensuring that the faith of every believer is rooted securely in Jesus Christ. Paul understood that the foundation of the Christian faith is not based on human wisdom, religious tradition, or good works, but on Christ alone—His life, death, and resurrection. This foundational truth was central to everything Paul preached and everything he built in the early church. As a master builder, Paul's responsibility was to ensure that every believer and every church he helped establish was firmly grounded in Christ, the only true foundation that can support the weight of eternal salvation, spiritual growth, and the hope of eternal life. In a world where false teachings, philosophies, and religious systems constantly threatened to lead people astray, Paul's unwavering commitment was to lay the foundation of Christ in every heart, knowing that anything built on another foundation would ultimately crumble. His words in this passage echo through the ages, reminding us that no matter how impressive or grand our lives, our churches, or our ministries may seem, if they are not built on Christ, they will not stand. Jesus Christ is the cornerstone, the bedrock of our faith, and Paul, as a faithful builder, devoted his entire life to making sure that this truth was at the center of everything.

Paul's declaration in 1 Corinthians 3:11 is not just a theological statement; it is a profound truth that speaks to the very heart of what it means to be a Christian. To build on Christ as the foundation means that our lives must be entirely centered on Him—on who He is, what He has done, and what He continues to do in and through us. Paul understood that the foundation determines the strength and stability of the entire structure. If the foundation is weak, everything built upon it will eventually fall. But if the foundation is strong, the building will stand firm, no matter what storms may come. Paul's life as a builder on Christ, the foundation, was characterized by his relentless focus on the Gospel of Jesus Christ. He never wavered from this foundation, never sought to build on anything else, and never compromised the truth of the Gospel for the sake of popularity or acceptance. He knew that only Christ could bear the weight of our sin, provide the grace we need for salvation, and offer the hope of eternal life. Paul's role as a builder was not to create something new or innovative but to lay the timeless, unshakable foundation of Christ in the hearts of believers, ensuring that their faith would stand the test of time and trials.

In 1 Corinthians 3:10, just before declaring Christ as the only foundation, Paul describes himself as a "wise masterbuilder" who has laid the foundation, and he warns others to "take heed how he buildeth thereupon." Paul knew that his work as a builder on Christ, the foundation, was of utmost importance, not just for his generation but for every generation to come. He wasn't interested in building temporary structures or superficial faith that would crumble under pressure. He was building for eternity, and that meant every stone, every truth, every teaching had to be aligned with the foundation of Christ. This is why Paul was so passionate about sound doctrine, about preaching Christ crucified, and about warning the church against false teachings that would lead them away from the true foundation. In Galatians 1:8, Paul writes, "But though we, or an angel from heaven, preach any other gospel unto you than that which we have preached unto you, let him be accursed." Paul's zeal for protecting the foundation of Christ was unwavering because he knew that the very salvation of souls was at stake. If people were led to build their lives on anything other than Christ—whether it be their own works, religious rituals, or human philosophies—they would ultimately be building on sand, and their faith would not stand.

To be a builder on Christ, the foundation, meant that Paul had to confront the false foundations that people were tempted to build upon. In the church at Corinth, as in many places where Paul ministered, there were factions, divisions, and disputes about leadership and doctrine. Some were saying, "I am of Paul," others, "I am of Apollos," and still others, "I am of Cephas" (1

Corinthians 1:12). But Paul quickly reminded them that neither he, nor Apollos, nor Cephas was the foundation of their faith—only Christ. In 1 Corinthians 3:5-7, Paul writes, "Who then is Paul, and who is Apollos, but ministers by whom ye believed, even as the Lord gave to every man? I have planted, Apollos watered; but God gave the increase. So then neither is he that planteth any thing, neither he that watereth; but God that giveth the increase." Paul's humility and clarity of purpose are evident in these words. He was not interested in building a personal following or making a name for himself. His sole focus was on building up the body of Christ on the true foundation of Jesus, ensuring that the church was united in Him, not divided by human allegiances or preferences.

As a builder on Christ, the foundation, Paul also understood that the materials we use in building matter. In 1 Corinthians 3:12-13, Paul warns that every person's work will be tested by fire: "Now if any man build upon this foundation gold, silver, precious stones, wood, hay, stubble; Every man's work shall be made manifest: for the day shall declare it, because it shall be revealed by fire; and the fire shall try every man's work of what sort it is." Paul's point is clear: while the foundation is Christ, what we build on that foundation must be worthy of Him. If we build with "wood, hay, and stubble"—that is, with things that are temporary, superficial, or rooted in human effort—our work will not endure. But if we build with "gold, silver, and precious stones"—things that are eternal, true, and aligned with the Gospel—our work will stand the test of time and be rewarded. Paul's life and ministry were a testament to building with materials that would last. He invested in people's lives, preaching the Gospel, teaching sound doctrine, and encouraging believers to grow in their faith. He knew that his work was not just for the present but for eternity, and he labored to ensure that what he built would withstand the fires of testing and remain for the glory of God.

Paul's role as a builder on Christ, the foundation, was also marked by his deep love and care for the church. He wasn't just a distant architect, drawing up plans and then leaving others to do the work. Paul was personally invested in the lives of the people he ministered to. He often referred to himself as a spiritual father to the churches he planted, and his letters are filled with expressions of deep affection, concern, and encouragement for the believers. In 1 Thessalonians 2:7-8, Paul writes, "But we were gentle among you, even as a nurse cherisheth her children: So being affectionately desirous of you, we were willing to have imparted unto you, not the gospel of God only, but also our own souls, because ye were dear unto us." Paul's role as a builder was not just about laying theological foundations; it was about building relationships, nurturing spiritual growth, and walking alongside believers as they grew in their faith. He cared deeply about the spiritual well-being of the church, and he labored tirelessly to ensure that they were rooted and grounded in Christ, able to withstand the challenges and trials they would inevitably face.

Paul's understanding of Christ as the foundation also shaped his approach to suffering and hardship. As a builder on Christ, the foundation, Paul knew that the Christian life was not free from trials, but he also knew that if our lives are built on Christ, we can withstand any storm. In 2 Corinthians 4:8-9, Paul writes, "We are troubled on every side, yet not distressed; we are perplexed, but not in despair; Persecuted, but not forsaken; cast down, but not destroyed." Paul's confidence in the face of suffering came from his deep assurance that Christ was his foundation. No matter what happened to him—whether imprisonment, beatings, or persecution—he knew that his life was built on the solid rock of Christ, and nothing could shake that foundation. This is the same confidence he wanted every believer to have. By building their lives on Christ, they too could stand firm in the midst of trials, knowing that their faith was secure in Him.

In conclusion, Paul's role as a Builder on Christ, the Foundation, as described in 1 Corinthians 3:11, was central to his life and ministry. He understood that Jesus Christ is the only foundation on which the Christian faith can be built, and he dedicated his life to ensuring that this foundation was laid in the hearts of believers. Paul's unwavering commitment to preaching Christ, protecting the Gospel from false teachings, and building up the church with materials that would last is an example for all of us. His life as a builder on Christ, the foundation, challenges us to examine our own lives and ministries, asking whether we are building on the true foundation of Christ or on something else. Paul's words remind us that only what is built on Christ will stand, and that we must take care to build with things that are eternal—truth, love, and faithfulness to the Gospel. As a builder on Christ, the foundation, Paul calls us to stand firm in the truth of the Gospel, to build our lives on the solid rock of Jesus, and to labor for His kingdom with the assurance that what is built on Christ will last for eternity. His legacy as a master builder on Christ continues to inspire and guide the church today, pointing us always to the one true foundation, Jesus Christ, our Lord and Savior.

Conclusion

In conclusion, "Paul: The Many Roles of a Servant of Christ" highlights the incredible ways that Paul served God, and his life serves as a blueprint for Christians today. Paul's journey from persecutor to apostle is a powerful reminder that no one is beyond the reach of God's grace. His roles as a preacher, teacher, shepherd, and defender of the faith show us the many ways that we, too, are called to serve. Paul didn't just preach the Gospel; he lived it every day, facing hardships, persecution, and suffering, yet never wavering in his commitment to Christ. As Christians, we are called to continue this mission, to be builders on Christ, the foundation, making sure our lives, families, and communities are grounded in Jesus. Like Paul, we are called to be spiritual warriors, standing firm in our faith against the spiritual battles we face. We are to be defenders of the faith, holding fast to the truth of God's Word and sharing it boldly with those around us. Paul's role as a shepherd reminds us to care for one another, to encourage and guide those who are new to the faith, and to be there for our fellow believers in times of need. His relentless commitment to spreading the Gospel challenges us to live with the same urgency, to preach the good news of salvation in every opportunity we have. Paul's endurance and perseverance teach us that no matter how difficult the journey may be, we are never alone—God is with us every step of the way. As we reflect on the many roles Paul played in the early church, we are reminded that we, too, have a part to play in building up God's kingdom. Through love, grace, courage, and faith, we can continue Paul's legacy by serving Christ with all our hearts, running the race set before us, and keeping the faith until the very end. Let Paul's example inspire us to live boldly for Christ, knowing that our labor in the Lord is never in vain.

Don't miss out!

Visit the website below and you can sign up to receive emails whenever Joshua Rhoades publishes a new book. There's no charge and no obligation.

https://books2read.com/r/B-A-AJLBB-LLPDF

BOOKS 2 READ

Connecting independent readers to independent writers.

Did you love *Paul- The Many Roles of a Servant of Christ*? Then you should read *A Christmas Journey of Faith*[1] by Joshua Rhoades!

In "A Christmas Journey of Faith", join four friends—Jake, Emma, Max, and Maya—on a thrilling time-travel adventure. When they discover a mysterious time machine hidden in an old shed, they embark on an incredible journey that takes them over 2,000 years into the past to witness the most important event in history: the birth of Jesus Christ. But this journey isn't just about seeing the past—it's about learning timeless lessons of faith, trust, and courage.

As they travel back to the time of Mary and Joseph, the friends witness the Christmas story unfold. From the angel Gabriel's visit to Mary to the long journey to Bethlehem and the miraculous birth of Jesus in a humble stable, they find themselves in the heart of the greatest miracle. They stand in awe as the shepherds receive the good news from the angels, follow the star with the wise men, and learn how Mary and Joseph trusted God's plan, even when it was difficult.

---

1. https://books2read.com/u/bWA9Qz

2. https://books2read.com/u/bWA9Qz

Each step of their journey shows how faith in God can guide us through life's challenges. The friends learn that Christmas isn't about presents or decorations, but about the gift of Jesus, who came to bring peace, love, and hope to the world. As they experience these incredible events, they realize that God's love and salvation are for everyone—rich or poor, young or old.

"A Christmas Journey of Faith" is a heartwarming story that reminds readers of all ages to trust God's plan and embrace the true meaning of Christmas. Through the eyes of Jake, Emma, Max, and Maya, readers will be inspired to live out the message of salvation and faith that Jesus brought to the world.

www.ingramcontent.com/pod-product-compliance
Lightning Source LLC
Chambersburg PA
CBHW051842130726
47987CB00002B/657